NON VIOLENCE

By the same author

Nuclear Holocaust and Christian Hope (with Richard K. Taylor)
Rich Christians in an Age of Hunger
Living More Simply (Ed.)

NON VIOLENCE

THE INVINCIBLE WEAPON?

RONALD J. SIDER

WORD PUBLISHING
Dallas · London · Sydney · Singapore

NON-VIOLENCE, THE INVINCIBLE WEAPON?

Non-Violence, The Invincible Weapon? was published under the title *Exploring the Limits of Non-Violence* by Hodder & Stoughton in 1988.

Library of Congress Cataloging-in-Publication Data

Sider, Ronald J.
  Non-violence, the invincible weapon? / Ronald J. Sider.
    p. cm.
  Bibliography: p.
  Includes index.
  ISBN 0-8499-3165-7 :
  1. Nonviolence—Religious aspects—Christianity. 2. Christianity and politics. I. Title.
BT736.15.S56   1989
241′.697—dc20   89-32821
                                                            CIP

Printed in the United States of America
9 8 0 1 2 3 9 AGF 9 8 7 6 5 4 3 2 1

CONTENTS

FOREWORD

Something strange is happening around the world. It is a quiet thing. It is a godly thing. It is an awesome thing. And nothing can stop it. It is a movement for peace. Unbelievable concessions toward demilitarization are being made by the Soviet Union. Leaders of the Palestinian people are offering to end a war of decades by recognizing the right of Israel to exist, if the Israeli government will recognize the Palestinian right to a homeland. In Central America, heads of state with diverse political ideologies are coming together in America and petitioning the superpowers to stay out of their countries and let them have the peace that the people of their nations crave.

Something wonderful is happening on college campuses across America. There are the stirrings of a new student movement that is challenging our youth to abandon their narcissistic lifestyles and sacrifice themselves for the good of others. At both Christian colleges and secular universities, I am witnessing the rudimentary traces of something that will rock our nation more profoundly than did the student movements of the sixties.

Everywhere there are voices crying in the wilderness, and they are crying for an end to destruction and death. The Prince of Peace is doing his thing. His Kingdom is at hand.

The overriding question which Christians must answer in the midst of this movement of the Spirit is what to do as these forces for peace and justice are unleashed.

Do we ride in the observation car at the end of the train, commenting on where history has taken us? Or do we sit in the locomotive, giving power and direction as society hurtles into God's future? Do we join the Lord in what he is doing in history? Or do we confine our religious efforts to preparing people for a salvation that lies outside of history?

I believe the Bible teaches us that Christians should be able to discern the signs of the times, and that we should be willing to join God as he works out his will in the world. I am convinced that the Scriptures have called us to join him in the struggle against those principalities and powers that would block the historical movement toward the Peaceable Kingdom.

That is why this book is so important. In it, Dr Ronald Sider outlines some of the history of the primary method which God wills for us to use in our struggle for justice and peace. He helps us see the incredible possibilities of non-violence as an instrument for social change.

From the time of the early church until the present, legions of Christians have stood against tyranny and oppression, armed only with the cross of Christ. Down through the corridors of time, there have been those who have changed history through valiant attempts to overcome evil with good. These cases are too numerous to list, and their influence is too great to measure. But the chronicles of history give ample evidence that non-violent social change can be victorious over those forces that command soldiers armed to the teeth. In this book, Dr Sider tells some of these stories and he does so with clarity and inspiration. He helps us to understand how those who have trusted in the Lord, rather than in war chariots, have made a difference in the destiny of our planet.

I was especially moved by his telling of the story of the non-violent revolution in the Philippines that culminated in the presidency of Corazon Aquino. I was moved because I knew Mrs Aquino's husband, Benigno. I met him a couple of years before his assassination on 21 August 1983. The two of us were speakers at a special conference on social change, sponsored by the Christian College Coalition in Washington, D.C. It was my lot to speak first at the gathering, and I talked about the relationship between love and power. I stressed the proposition that love expressed in sacrifice is at the heart of the gospel, and that love will ultimately triumph over those who exercise power in the cause of evil.

As I spoke, I noticed an Oriental man sitting in the front row of the audience. He had tears streaming down his cheeks. Not yet having been introduced to him, I did not know that this man was Benigno Aquino, the exiled senator from the Philippines, and the chief opponent to the dictator, Ferdinand Marcos. I only knew him to be a man who was emotionally resonating to the declaration that "love never faileth."

When my lecture was over, Senator Aquino came up and embraced me. And he said, in words I will never forget, "I am convinced that you are right. I am going to return to my country and confront the power of Marcos with the love of God. I may die. But the love of God which I express shall prevail." The rest, as they say, is history.

It is not simply the belief that non-violent sacrificial love works that entices me to embrace it as the basis for all attempts to change the world. It is that I am convinced that God, in Christ, has ordained us to go this route—even if it means crucifixion. It is not because pragmatism suggests it, but because the Lord commands it, that I embrace it. However, I am not sure where my heart is on this matter. On the intellectual level, I am convinced that any reading of the teachings of Christ will warrant a non-violent philosophy of social action. But I am not sure of what I would do if I or my family were threatened with violence from obscene conquerors. I must think through the cost of non-violence and prepare myself for their coming. I must learn of Christ and I must be broken and remade into one who can carry a cross. This book is helping me to do just that.

Perhaps what makes this book so special is that there are, in it, some realistic suggestions as to what people like me, who believe in non-violent social change, can do to work out their beliefs in concrete terms. Specifically, the suggestion that those of us who believe in non-violence bind ourselves together into *Christian Peacemaker Teams,* seems promising. Dr Sider proposes that such groups could patrol lines of demarkation between warring peoples, deterring invasions. They could deny access to certain towns or buildings under attack (as the Witness for Peace people have done in Nicaragua). They could separate hostile groups (as a Quaker team did during the struggle of Native Americans at Wounded Knee).

I can envision people, especially young people, joining such peace brigades in the years to come. And I believe that this little book could inspire many to the kind of radical discipleship that can make non-violence in this form an instrument of hope for the future.

Theologically, I have never been one of those postmillennialists who believe that the kingdom of God can be realized before the Second Coming of Christ. With the cynic, I quote with regularity the words of Jesus who said that there would be wars and rumors of wars. However, I am also convinced that God has already begun to create his kingdom in the here and now, and that he wishes to work through each of us to that end. I believe that he wants to begin in us his good work which he will complete at the day of his return. Thus, I hold that the peace which shall be completed at the eschaton is a peace that he is beginning to create through his people even now, in the midst of the tensions of this present age. Dr Sider's call is a call to be submissive to this movement of the Lord and to become people through whom the work of his peace can be accomplished. In the spirit of non-violence, Dr Sider wants to help us to pray the Lord's Prayer and say, "Thy Kingdom come, thy will be done, on earth, as it is in heaven." Those peacemakers who would pray that prayer will welcome this book.

Anthony Campolo

INTRODUCTION

There are only two invincible forces in the twentieth century—the atom bomb and nonviolence.

Bishop Leonidas Proano of Ecuador[1]

What good would it do for three kayaks, three canoes and a rubber dinghy to paddle into the path of a Pakistani steamship? Or for a tiny fishing boat with unarmed, praying Americans aboard to sail towards an American battleship threatening Nicaragua? Or for an eighty-year-old lady in a wheelchair to stop in front of advancing Filipino tanks?

The tanks stopped and a non-violent revolution succeeded. The American battleship left and the threat of invasion faded. And the US shipment of arms to Pakistan stopped.

A need for exploration

Those were just three of the more dramatic successes of non-violent confrontation in the last two decades. Everyone, of course, knows how Mahatma Gandhi's non-violent revolution defeated the British Empire and how Martin Luther King, Jr's peaceful civil-rights crusade changed American history. There are many more cases of non-violent victories over dictatorship and oppression in the last one hundred years. In fact, Harvard's Dr Gene Sharp, the foremost student of non-violence today, says that the twentieth century has seen a remarkable expansion of the substitution of non-violent struggle for violence.[2]

Surely that fact suggests a crucial area of urgent exploration in the late twentieth century. No one living in the most bloody century in human history needs to be reminded of the horror of war. A violent sword has devoured a hundred million people in a mere hundred years. The mushroom cloud reminds us of greater agony yet to come unless we find alternative ways to resolve international conflict. A method that destroys a hundred million people in one century and threatens to wipe out far more is hardly a model of success. From the ordinary layperson to the most highly placed general, it is obvious that the search for peaceful alternatives is a practical necessity.

It is also a moral demand. Christians in the just war tradition (a majority since the fourth century) have always argued that killing must be a last resort. All realistic alternatives must first be tried before one resorts to war. In a century where Gandhi, King and a host of others have demonstrated that non-violence works, how can Christians in the just war tradition claim that the violence they justify is truly a last resort until they have invested billions and trained tens of thousands of people in a powerful, sustained testing of the possibilities of non-violent alternatives?

Pacifists have long claimed that there is an alternative to violence. How can their words have integrity unless they are ready to risk death in a massive non-violent confrontation with the bullies and tyrants that swagger through human history?

In short, the concrete victories of modern non-violent campaigns, the spiralling dangers of lethal weapons and the moral demands of Christian faith all focus a clear imperative. It is time for the Christian church—indeed all people of faith—to explore, in a more sustained and sophisticated way than ever before in human history, what can be done non-violently.

That does not mean that one must be a pacifist to engage in serious exploration of the possibilities of non-violence. One can conclude reluctantly that we still must possess nuclear weapons and at the same time fervently desire to substitute non-violent for violent strategies wherever possible. This book does not deal at all with the old debate between pacifists and just war theorists—precisely because that debate need not be settled for both to join together in a new, sustained testing of the possibilities of nonviolence.

The purpose of this book is to promote that exploration. The first chapter briefly surveys the history of non-violent action. The next two chapters tell the story of two very recent, dramatic, non-violent campaigns. Chapters four and five plead for action—now.

Preliminary definitions

But first, a brief word on terminology and scope. Non-violence is not passive non-resistance. Nor is coercion always violent. Non-lethal coercion (as in a boycott or peaceful march) that respects the integrity and personhood of the 'opponent' is not immoral or violent.[3] By non-violence, I mean an activist confrontation with evil that respects the personhood even of the 'enemy' and therefore seeks both to end the oppression and reconcile the oppressor.

Non-violence refers to a vast variety of methods or strategies. It includes things from verbal and symbolic persuasion through social, economic and political non-cooperation (including boycotts and strikes) to even more confrontational intervention. Dr Gene Sharp describes 198 different non-violent tactics in his classic analysis of the varieties of non-violent action.[4] This book does not focus exclusively on any one strategy. Concrete situations demand their unique mix of tactics.

Possibilities worth considering

The arenas where non-violent alternatives might possibly (at least to a great degree) replace lethal violence are basically threefold: police work at the micro level; national self-defense and international, governmental peacekeeping at the macro level; and a wide variety of middle-level situations demanding conflict resolution, from guerrilla warfare to religious conflict in a society to revolution against a dictator. I believe we ought to explore the possibilities of nonviolence for all three of these areas.[5] This book, however, focuses largely on the third area.

In their peace pastoral letter, the US Catholic bishops said that 'nonviolent means of resistance to evil deserve much more study and consideration than they have thus far received. There have been significant instances in which people have successfully resisted oppression without recourse to arms.'[6] I turn now to that story of heroic struggle and astounding success.

PART I:

A GROWING VISION

1   WHAT EXISTS IS POSSIBLE

Boulding's First Law says: 'What exists is possible.'[1]
From before the time of Christ to the present, hundreds
of successful instances of non-violent action have occurred. Often spontaneous, and seldom organised,
courageous non-violent protest, non-cooperation and
intervention have stopped brutal dictators, quelled
raging mobs and overthrown foreign conquerors.[2]

The full story of unarmed daring has yet to be
written.[3] Here I do not try to fill that gap, for that would
require a vast library rather than a brief chapter.
Rather, I outline a few historical illustrations of non-
violent direct action in order to show how an alternative
vision for resolving social conflict has emerged.

Two Examples from the First Century

In AD 26, Pontius Pilate, the new Roman Governor of
Judea, outraged the Jews by bringing military standards emblazoned with the Emperor's image into
Jerusalem. Since Jewish belief condemned all rep-
resentation of the human form, the religious leaders
begged Pilate to remove the ensigns from the holy city.
What happened is best told by the first-century Jewish
historian, Josephus:

> Hastening after Pilate to Caesarea, the Jews implored him
> to remove the standards from Jerusalem and to uphold the
> laws of their ancestors. When Pilate refused, they fell

prostrate around his house and for five whole days and nights remained motionless in that position. On the ensuing day Pilate took his tribunal in the great stadium, and summoning the multitude, with apparent intention of answering them, gave the arranged signal to his armed soldiers to surround the Jews. Finding themselves in a ring of troops, three deep, the Jews were struck dumb at this unexpected sight. Pilate, after threatening to cut them down, if they refused to admit Caesar's images, signaled to the soldiers to draw their swords. Thereupon the Jews, as by concerted action, flung themselves in a body on the ground, extended their necks, and exclaimed that they were ready rather to die than to transgress the law. Overcome with astonishment at such intense religious zeal, Pilate gave orders for the immediate removal of the standards from Jerusalem.[4]

Non-violent intervention had worked!

A few years later, the Jews won an even more striking non-violent victory. Caligula was the first Roman Emperor to require that his subjects worship him as a god during his lifetime. In AD 39, Caligula sent Petronius to Jerusalem with three legions of soldiers to install his statue in the temple in Jerusalem. Outraged, the Jews organised a primitive version of a nationwide strike. Refusing to plant crops, tens of thousands of Jews took part in a 'sit-in' in front of the residence of the Roman legate, Petronius. For forty days they protested non-violently. Jewish leaders summoned for private persuasion remained firmly united with their people. They would all rather die, they insisted, than permit such a desecration of their temple.

This courage and commitment so impressed Petronius that he decided to risk his life and ask the Emperor to change his mind. Caligula was furious. He sent a messenger commanding Petronius to commit suicide. Very soon after dispatching this messenger, however, Caligula himself was murdered. Fortunately strong winds delayed the emperor's messenger, who arrived with his fatal letter twenty-seven days *after* Petronius had learnt that Caligula was dead.[5]

Non-violent direct action had succeeded again.

Attila and the Pope

In the middle of the fifth century, the conquering Attila marched to the very gates of the 'Eternal City'. Having swept through central and eastern Europe in a bloody campaign, Attila hungered for the ultimate prize – Rome. His reputation preceded him. Terrified Romans believed that '... the grass never grew on the spot where his horse had trod'.[6] Facing this powerful warrior stood a demoralised Roman army and a daring Roman bishop.

Some stories portray Pope Leo I riding a mule, leading a small group towards Attila's advancing army. Armed only with a crucifix and a papal crown, the brave Leo allegedly directs his men in song as they advance. Finally, they face the enemy – their backs to the Roman wall, their exposed fronts to the 'barbarians'. Now the incredible happens. Attila, alarmed and confused, turns tail and runs – never to be seen again![7] Non-violent peacekeeping at its pristine best? Perhaps, although many of the details are probably legendary.

But modern historians do believe that Leo the Great, accompanied by a Roman Senator and other official ambassadors, did confront the invading Hun. Whether the negotiators were unarmed, singing and riding on mules is open to doubt. What *is* certain is the success of the mission. According to Gibbon, in his classic work on the Roman Empire, 'The pressing eloquence of Leo, his majestic aspect and sacerdotal robes, excited the veneration of Attila for the spiritual father of the Christians.'[8] The two parties managed to hammer out an acceptable treaty. The invading army withdrew.[9] Leo the Great's willingness to intervene directly and face a brutal warrior with overwhelming military might probably saved Rome from destruction.

Neglected History

Over the intervening centuries, there were undoubtedly examples of non-violent action. Unfortunately, that history has attracted fewer historians than the bloody battles of the Charlemagnes and Napoleons. But one should not assume from the relative silence of the history books that these centuries were free from any form of non-violent resistance.

The American Revolution offers a striking illustration of this historical oversight. Almost every American knows about General Washington and his military victories in the War of Independence. Only a very few realise how successful non-violent resistance to British tyranny had been even before a shot had been fired. But a scholarly study just published demonstrates that by 1775 nine of the American colonies had already won *de facto* independence by non-violent means.[10]

The non-violent struggle in Hungary in the latter part of the nineteenth century is another exciting, yet relatively unknown, chapter in the emerging history of non-violent action. Between 1850 and 1867, Hungarians resisted Austrian imperialism non-violently and eventually succeeded without violence after armed revolt had failed miserably. In 1849 Austria crushed a popular, violent Hungarian rebellion against Austrian domination. The next year, however, a prominent lawyer, Ferencz Deàk, led the whole country into non-violent resistance. Church leaders disobeyed Austrian orders. People refused to pay Austrian taxes, boycotted Austrian goods, and ostracised Austrian troops. So successful was the non-violent resistance that *The Times* of London declared in an editorial on 24 August 1861: 'Passive resistance can be so organized as to become more troublesome than armed rebellion.'[11] In 1866 and 1867, Austria agreed to reopen the Hungarian parliament and restore the constitution.[12]

Far away in the Andes mountains, another non-violent victory occurred in the nineteenth century. In his book *Warriors of Peace*, Lanza del Vasto describes the incident this way:

> When relations between Argentina and Chile deteriorated, the two armies marched toward each other through the high passes in the Andes. But on each side, a bishop went ahead of the troops. The bishops met and exchanged the kiss of peace in the sight of the soldiers. And instead of fighting, they sealed a pact of alliance and perpetual friendship between the two nations. A statue of Christ, His hand raised in blessing, stands on the mountain to commemorate this victimless victory.[13]

By courageously placing themselves between two opposing armies, these peacekeeping bishops doubtless averted bloodshed.

A Growing Vision

As Dr Gene Sharp of Harvard's Program on Nonviolent Sanctions has pointed out, the twentieth century has witnessed an astonishing increase in the use of non-violence.[14] Some of the key figures are household names around the world: America's Martin Luther King, Jr,

India's Mahatma Gandhi, Poland's Lech Walesa, the Philippines' Cory Aquino. Many more are less familiar. But all have contributed significantly to a growing awareness of non-violent alternatives.

A Brazilian soldier named Colonel Rondon is one of the less well-known heroes. By the early 1900s, the Chavante Indian nation was violently resisting its Brazilian oppressors. The hatred and brutality were mutual. But Colonel (later General) Rondon, an officer in Brazil's army, determined to deal with the Chavante nation in a radically new, non-violent, way. Rejecting the 'Shoot the Indians on sight!' policy of the past, Rondon instructed his men, 'Die if you must, but never kill an Indian.'[15]

Success did not come overnight. Members of Rondon's peacekeeping force were wounded – some severely. Yet the 'Indian Protective Service' organised by Rondon lived up to its name. Finally, in 1946, the Brazilian government signed a treaty with the Chavante people. Rondon's protective service had taken no Indian lives since its founding some forty years earlier.[16] The treaty permitted the construction of a communication system through the Chavante's jungle home, over which General Rondon telegraphed a friend, 'This is a victory of patience, suffering and love.'[17]

While Rondon experimented with peacekeeping in the field, philosophers expounded it in the public forum. In 1910, the pragmatist William James published 'The Moral Equivalent of War'. In his article, he proposes the conscription of young people for a war against 'nature' and for social welfare.[18] James had little time for idealistic visions, suggesting that:

> Pacifists ought to enter more deeply into the aesthetical and ethical point of view of their opponents. So long as antimilitarists propose no substitute for war's disciplinary

function, no *moral equivalent* of war . . . so long they fail to realize the full inwardness of the situation. And as a rule they do fail. The duties, penalties, and sanctions pictured in the utopias they paint are all too weak and tame to touch the military-minded.[19]

To be fair, James was not advocating a new 'peace army'. He simply saw his plan as having tremendous social value. Yet many today view James' essay as the antecedent of the modern peacekeeping force concept.[20]

Mahatma Gandhi, Badshah Khan, and the Defeat of the British Empire

The philosophers of the West, however, are over-shadowed by the 'Great-Soul' of the East – Mahatma Gandhi. Gandhi first began work on the idea of a non-violent army while in South Africa in 1913. But his skeletal proposal took on flesh in 1922, when Gandhi organised a corps of peace volunteers in Bombay, India.[21] The next ten years witnessed a disciplined and growing satyagraha ('truth-force').[22] During the year-long civil disobedience of 1930, they engaged in direct, albeit non-violent, confrontation with British colonialism. Thousands of peaceful protesters suffered savage police attacks.

An American journalist, Negley Farson, recorded the following story of a volunteer Sikh repeatedly bloodied by a British officer:

> [The police sergeant was] . . . so sweaty from his exertions that his Sam Browne [a leather belt] had stained his white tunic. I watched him with my heart in my mouth. He drew back his arm for a final swing – and then he dropped his hands down by his side. 'It's no use,' he said, turning to me with half an apologetic grin, 'You can't hit a bugger when he stands up to you like that!' He gave the Sikh a mock salute and walked off.[23]

Eventually, of course, Gandhi's non-violent soldiers defeated the British Empire. Rather than retell this classic non-violent victory, however, I will focus on one largely unfamiliar strand of the non-violent struggle for Indian independence.

In the annals of non-violent intervention, no episode is more astonishing than that of Badshah Khan and his non-violent army of eighty thousand Muslim Pathans.[24] The Pathans lived in the strategic Khyber Pass, the north-west gateway to India from Afghanistan and Russia. The British who tried to subdue them considered the Pathans the most savage, brutal warriors they had ever met. The Pathans' strict code of revenge obligated them to avenge the slightest insult. For a Pathan, the surest road to Paradise was to die 'with his rifle smoking'.[25] India's future Prime Minister, Jawaharlal Nehru, commented that the Pathan male, 'loved his gun better than his child or brother'.[26]

When Badshah Khan persuaded the Pathans to adopt non-violence, even Gandhi was amazed. 'That such men,' Gandhi exclaimed, 'who would have killed a human being with no more thought than they would kill a sheep or a hen, should at the bidding of one man have laid down their arms and accepted non-violence as the superior weapon sounds almost like a fairy tale.'[27]

But they did. Badshah Khan was a Pathan Muslim who became enthralled with Gandhi's vision of non-violent struggle for freedom. Khan began to dream of 'an army of nonviolent soldiers, directed and disciplined, with officers, cadres, uniforms, a flag'.[28] Calling his volunteers the 'Servants of God', Khan organised 'the first professional nonviolent army'.[29] They marched and drilled, wore a special uniform (a red shirt), and developed a careful organisational structure complete with officers – and a bagpipe corps! They also worked in the villages, opened schools, and maintained order at public gatherings.

Badshah Khan's non-violent army was ready when the Congress Party issued its historic declaration of non-violence in the struggle for Indian independence on 31 December 1929:

> We recognize, however, that the most effective way of gaining our freedom is not through violence. We will prepare ourselves by withdrawing, so far as we can, all voluntary association from the British government, and will prepare for civil disobedience, including the nonpayment of taxes. We are convinced that if we can but withdraw our voluntary help, stop payment of the taxes, without doing violence even under provocation, the end of this inhuman rule is assured.[30]

In April 1930 the great Salt Campaign began. The British government monopolised the sale of salt, and also taxed it. With Gandhi in the lead, millions of Indians broke the salt laws, illegally buying and selling millions of pounds of salt.

The British response was brutal. Soldiers beat unarmed protesters with steel-tipped staffs. They raided the offices of the Congress Party. One hundred thousand Indians landed in jail.

Nowhere was the repression as bad as in Badshah Khan's home in the strategic north-west frontier. When he called his Pathan people to non-violent resistance, Khan was quickly arrested. Non-violent civil disobedience promptly broke out everywhere among the Pathans. Bayonets and bullets were the British response. On one bloody afternoon, they killed over two hundred unarmed protesters and wounded many more.

One incredible scene involved the Garhwal Rifles, crack Indian troops commanded by British officers. When they saw unarmed men, women and children being slaughtered, they refused to obey orders to shoot. 'You may blow us from your guns, if you like,' they told their British commanders, 'but we will not shoot our unarmed brethren.'[31]

British brutality evoked massive support for the Pathans. In a very short time, Khan's non-violent army swelled to eighty thousand volunteers. Fearing this Pathan non-violence even more than their former savagery, the British did everything to destroy the 'Red Shirts' and provoke them to violence. They ordered them to strip naked in public and beat them into unconsciousness when they refused. After public humiliation, many were thrown into pools of human excrement. Everywhere, the British hunted Badshah Khan's non-violent army like animals. But the proud Pathans remained firmly non-violent.[32]

Throughout the rest of India, too, the non-violent struggle and the brutal repression raged on throughout 1930. Finally, at the end of the year, the British government summoned Gandhi to arrange a truce. For the first time, the British recognised and negotiated with Gandhi's non-violent movement for independence.

Of course, the struggle for freedom was not yet over. For the next decade and a half, Badshah Khan and his non-violent Red Shirts played a key role in the battle for independence. Always they worked for peace and reconciliation. In 1946, when thousands died in Hindu–Muslim violence, ten thousand of Khan's Servants of God protected Hindu and Sikh minorities in the northwest frontier and eventually restored order in the large city of Peshawar.[33] Finally, in 1947, Gandhi's campaign of non-violent intervention wrested Indian independence from the British Empire. Badshah Khan's peaceful army of Pathan Red Shirts deserved a good deal of the credit.

This story of non-violent direct action by Muslim Pathans with a long history of brutal violence is one of the most amazing chapters in the development of an alternative path to resolve social conflict. Khan's biographer is surely correct: 'If Badshah Khan could raise a non-violent army of a people so steeped in violence as the Pathans, there is no country on earth where it cannot be done.'[34] Perhaps Gandhi's insistence that non-violence is meant for the strong helps explain the Pathan's success. When Badshah Khan asked Gandhi why the Pathans grasped the idea of non-violence more quickly than the Hindus, Gandhi responded: 'Non-violence is not for cowards. It is for the brave, the courageous. And the Pathans are more brave and courageous than the Hindus.'[35]

Gandhi and Badshah Khan redefined courage. Towards the end of his life, this incredible liberator of India remarked:

> My non-violence does not admit of running away from danger and leaving dear ones unprotected. Between violence and cowardly flight, I can only prefer violence to cowardice. I can no more preach non-violence to a coward than I can tempt a blind man to enjoy healthy scenes. Non-violence is the summit of bravery. And in my own experience, I have had no difficulty in demonstrating to men trained in the school of violence the superiority of non-violence.[36]

Developments Between the Wars

In other parts of the world, too, non-violence was discussed and tested in the Twenties and Thirties.

In 1920, the Germans used non-violence successfully to defeat a *coup d'état*. On 13 March 1920, right-wing troops seized Berlin, the capital of Germany, and declared a new government. Spontaneously, tens of thousands of Berliners began a strike. The next day, a ringing call for a general strike echoed throughout Germany:

> The strongest resistance is required. No enterprise must work as long as the military dictatorship reigns. Therefore, stop working! Strike! Strangle the reactionary clique! Fight by all means to uphold the Republic. Put all mutual discords aside. There is only one way to prevent Wilhelm II from returning: the whole economy must be paralysed! No hand must move! No proletarian must help the military dictatorship. The total general strike must be carried through![37]

Even though some workers were shot, almost everyone went on strike. The bureaucracy refused to run the government. Within four days, the leader (Wolfgang Kapp) fled to Sweden and the rebellion collapsed. Even though the police and army had failed to resist the coup, even though the coup succeeded and the rebels seized the machinery of government, they were unable to govern. Why? Because the people would not obey. Massive non-violent resistance had defeated armed soldiers.[38]

In the Thirties, James' idea of a 'peace army' took one small step towards reality. When Japan invaded Manchuria in 1931, the League of Nations demonstrated its weakness by doing almost nothing. Even when the Chinese launched a total boycott of Japanese goods and Japan responded with brutal repression, the League failed to respond. At this juncture an amazing letter appeared in the London *Daily Express*. Signed by three well-known churchpeople (the woman preacher, A. Maude Royden, Canon H. R. C. 'Dick' Sheppard, and Dr A. Herbert Grey), the letter urged: 'Men and women who believe it to be their duty should volunteer to place themselves unarmed between the combatants [in China] . . . We have written to the League of Nations offering ourselves for service in such a Peace Army.'[39] The League Secretary, General Eric Drummond, responded quickly, noting that the League Constitution prohibited consideration of 'private' proposals. At the same time, however, he promised to circulate the idea among the press in Geneva.[40] Editorials mushroomed worldwide. 'The suggestion that such an army might suitably interpose itself between the forces of two peoples at war is both intelligent and apt,' remarked the Manchester *Guardian*.[41] Across the ocean, *Time* magazine scoffed at foolish 'Occidentals willing to go to Shanghai and heroically interpose themselves between the fighting Orientals . . .'[42]

Back in Britain, however, the proposal gained support. Brigadier General Frank Percy Crozier – a decorated veteran of the Western Front – volunteered almost immediately.[43] Approximately eight hundred others followed, forming an organisation called 'The Peace Army'.[44] The Army, unfortunately, existed mostly on paper and never actually served in Shanghai. Still, a precedent had been set. The proposal for a 'peace army' had drawn marked attention, and fire, from around the world.

Battling Hitler Non-violently

Brave appeals for a non-violent peace army did not however prevent the planet from slipping into the most deadly world war in human history. But even in those years, indeed precisely in many of the countries under the brutal thumb of Adolf Hitler, non-violence persisted and grew.

Hitler easily conquered Norway and established
Vidkun Quisling as his puppet in 1940.[45] But when
Quisling tried to establish fascist institutions, massive
non-violent civil disobedience erupted. Teachers risked
their lives, refusing to teach fascist propaganda. Labour
unions struck and sabotaged machinery, even though
their leaders were imprisoned and killed. Almost all the
Lutheran clergy resigned from the state church which
Quisling tried to control. When the Gestapo demanded
that the Catholic Archbishop withdraw his signature
from a letter supporting the defiant Lutheran clergy, he
replied: 'You can take my head, but not my signature.'[46]
Quisling failed in his attempt to impose fascism
through the schools and church.

Norwegians succeeded in saving more than half of the
country's Jews. And resistance was even more successful in this regard in Denmark, Finland and Bulgaria.[47]
A secret tip-off concerning the impending arrest of
Danish Jews enabled the Danes to hide and then
smuggle ninety-three percent of the Danish Jews to
neutral Sweden. Although allied with Germany, Finland refused to deport their Jews, even when Hitler's
chief of security police threatened to cut off Finland's
food supply. 'We would rather perish together with the
Jews,' Finland's Foreign Minister told the astonished
Heinrich Himmler.[48]

Also a German ally, Bulgaria initially passed anti-
Jewish legislation. But massive resistance to anti-
Jewish measures emerged at every level of society, from
peasant to priest. The Metropolitan of the Belgian
Orthodox Church hid the Chief Rabbi in his home.
Another Orthodox bishop told the Bulgarian king he
would lead a massive campaign of civil disobedience
against deportation, 'including personally lying down
on the railroad tracks before the deportation trains'.[49]

Not one of the fifty thousand Bulgarian Jews fell into Hitler's hands.

Overthrowing Dictators

Non-violence toppled two dictators in Central America in 1944. General Martinez seized power in El Salvador in 1931.[50] The next year, he savagely crushed a peasant revolt, killing thousands of persons. For thirteen years, the tyrannical autocrat ruled. In early 1944, he put down a revolt, torturing some and killing others. In response, university students spread the idea of a non-violent general strike. Within two weeks, doctors, lawyers, engineers, teachers, shopkeepers and railway workers all left their posts. The economy ground to a halt. After a short period, Martinez resigned and fled to Guatemala, where he explained his resignation:

> In the first few days of April, I defeated the seditionaries with arms, but recently they provoked a strike. Then I no longer wanted to fight. Against whom was I going to fire? Against children and against youths...? Women also were enlisted in the movement and in this way I no longer had an objective at which to fire.[51]

General Jorge Ubico had ruled Guatemala with an iron fist since 1931. Unfortunately for him, when El Salvador's dictator fled to Guatemala in May 1944, he brought along a contagious example of non-violent resistance. The widespread opposition to Ubico's tyranny took heart. First students, then school teachers, went on strike. When the cavalry charged a silent procession of women and killed a school teacher, a total strike occurred in the capital, Guatemala City. Workers struck. Businesses and offices closed. The streets were deserted. On 1 July 1944 Ubico also gave up.[52]

Nor are the victories in El Salvador and Guatemala isolated examples. Non-violent general strikes have overthrown at least seven Latin American dictators in the twentieth century.[53]

Although finally unsuccessful, massive non-violent resistance to the Russian invasion of Czechoslovakia in 1968 denied the Soviets an early victory. The Russians had assumed that their half a million Warsaw Pact troops would overwhelm the Czechs and install a puppet government in days. But near-unanimous non-violent resistance on the part of the Czech people preserved the government of the reform-minded Alexander Dubček for eight months.[54] A decade and a half later, Solidarity in Poland again used non-violent techniques against Soviet totalitarianism. And again the people failed to achieve genuine freedom. But, with hardly any loss of life, they were able to achieve astonishing change for a short time. Even after the clampdown, substantial accomplishments remained.

Professor Gene Sharp, Director of the Program on Nonviolent Sanctions at Harvard notes:

> Each successive case of nonviolent anti-communist struggle in Eastern Europe since 1953 has been more difficult for the Soviets to crush. Resistance in East Germany in June, 1953, was crushed in two days. The improvised Czech-Slovak resistance in 1968–69 ultimately failed, but it held off Soviet control for eight months, which would have been impossible by military means. In Poland, resistance continues after five years with major achievements, including a large illegal information system that publishes papers, magazines and books.[55]

The Philippines Revolution of 1986 is of course the most recent, the most famous, and the most successful example of non-violent overthrow of dictatorship. But that story will have to wait for chapter three.

Peacekeeping by the United Nations

Since UN peacekeeping forces regularly carry weapons, their story does not actually belong in this book. But they are relevant to our theme for several reasons. Relying largely on moral power, they often never fired a shot. Their existence witnesses to the growing desire for a transnational, less violent solution to the vicious wars that modern nation-states so often fight. Thus they reflect and point to a yearning for a non-violent alternative to war. A brief overview of the UN's peacekeeping forces is therefore appropriate.

The UN, like the League of Nations before it, made no provision for peacekeeping in its charter. According to UN diplomat Brian Urquhart (Undersecretary-General for Special Political Affairs), discovering peacekeeping was 'like penicillin . . . We came across it while looking for something else.'[56] In late 1946, a special UN diplomatic commission investigated the unrest in northern Greece. Military aid from nearby communist countries (Albania, Bulgaria and Yugoslavia) was pouring across the border to likeminded guerrillas. The commission requested observation and conciliation assistance – though a speedy victory by the Greek government ended both the crisis and eventually the commission.[57]

Still, a precedent had been set. In 1948, the then Secretary-General Trygve Lie proposed a 'UN Guard' – basically a professional, international police force. Unfortunately, his novel concept was a quick casualty of the Cold War.[58] Yet Ralph Bunche (later Undersecretary-General) pursued the concept of UN peacekeeping, an idea soon put to the test by Arab–Israeli armistice efforts in 1948–1949. Following Bunche's mediation of the cease-fire, military observers were sent to the Middle East to monitor the armistice.[59] It was the first of many UN commitments.[60]

A series of flash points followed in quick succession. In 1949, UN observers arrived on the India–Pakistan border to police the demarcation line following the Kashmir cease-fire.[61] Multinational troops under the UN banner carried out full-scale military operations in Korea (1950–1953). Actual UN troops landed in the Middle East in late 1956 to help extricate the British and French armies from Egypt and the Israeli army from the Sinai. In 1958, six hundred UN military observers were sent to Beirut, facilitating the withdrawal of US troops. Two years later, twenty thousand UN troops descended on the Congo (now Zaire) – a newly independent African nation caught in the East–West crossfire. In 1962, a Pakistani contingent of limited size and mandate moved into West Irian (formerly Dutch East Indies), for a one-year period.[62]

An accurate appraisal of these first fifteen years of UN peacekeeping remains difficult. In some ways, in fact, the verdict is still out. What *is* clear is the complex character of UN missions. Most involved a curious mixture of pacific persuasion and violence, ranging from Kashmir to Korea. Peacekeepers often struggled, however, to minimise violence and maximise reconciliation. The failures are well known, the successes often obscured.

To their credit, UN peacekeepers have honestly confronted past errors in judgement. The euphemistic 'police action' of Korea, for example, is unlikely to be repeated. Speaking at Harvard University in June 1963, then Secretary-General U Thant declared, 'The idea that conventional military methods – or, to put it bluntly, war – can be used by or on behalf of the United Nations to counter aggression and secure the peace, seems now to be rather impractical.'[63] The massive commitment of troops seen in the Congo, likewise, remains equally unpopular in many quarters. The costs are simply too high and the returns often minimal.

Yet stories abound of successful – and non-violent – UN peacekeeping efforts. In the Congo, for instance, UN troops attempted repeatedly to downplay violence. Antony Gilpin (former Deputy-Chief of Civilian Operations) tells the true story of a unique rescue mission. Sudanese UN troops had been surrounded and were under shelling attack. According to Gilpin, a Nigerian *police band* '. . . marched through the lines and, under cover of martial music, led out the beleaguered Sudanese'.[64] Non-violent peacekeeping at its artistic best!

UN observers acted just as creatively (if not artistically) in Kashmir. There, the India–Pakistan border suffered repeated firefights between hot-headed soldiers. Gene Keyes quotes a memorable story of UN intervention:

> One observer who had witnessed a confrontation between an Indian and a Pakistani patrol jumped into his UN marked jeep as the two groups started shooting at each other and drove into the path of fire with the UN flag flying from his vehicle. Both patrols ceased firing, and with the arrival of more observers the fighting stopped.[65]

Once again, non-violent peacekeeping proved powerful and effective.

In the more traditional UN border actions, reviews have been mixed. In West Irian, the mandate was clear and limited. UN troops were there simply to bridge the gap between the Dutch withdrawal and the arrival of the Indonesians.[66] Their mission lasted approximately one year and was largely successful. The Middle East has proven more difficult. The 'United Nations

Emergency Force' (UNEF), established in 1956, served for over ten years. During that time, it engaged in a number of significant peacekeeping initiatives. Major General Indar Jit Rikhye (Ret.), commander of the UNEF in the late 1960s, details some of those accomplishments in his recent article 'Peacekeeping and Peacemaking':

> The [UN] peacekeepers were required to supervise the withdrawal of foreign forces from Egyptian territory, to provide security for the canal clearance operations, and to interpose themselves between the Egyptian and Israeli forces during the latter's phased withdrawal. On completion of these tasks, UNEF was deployed between the Egyptians and the Israelis along the armistice demarcation line in the Gaza Strip and along the international frontier in the Sinai. Furthermore, UNEF was made responsible to ensure the freedom of shipping through the Straits of Tiran.[67]

In 1967, however, the Egyptian President, Gamal Abdel Nasser, moved his troops dangerously close to the Israeli border and demanded a UN pull-out from U Thant. The UN complied and Egyptian forces were routed in the ensuing six-day war. Thant's decision was probably legally correct (based on the 1956 negotiations), but it was politically disastrous. Then Israeli Foreign Minister, Abba Eban, exclaimed, 'U Thant folded the umbrella just when the rain began to fall.'[68] Israel's chief ally, the United States, also complained. But the decision to withdraw had been made.

The UN pull-out would not last long, however. Following the 1973 Middle East War, the blue-helmeted troops returned to the Sinai (UNEF II) and took up new positions in the Golan Heights between Israeli and Syrian Forces (UNDOF).[69] In 1978, additional UN forces moved into southern Lebanon (UNIFIL).[70] UN presence in the Middle East continues to this day.[71]

Other border hot-spots have periodically boiled over. In 1965, war broke out between India and Pakistan, and additional UN observers moved in to beef up the original force established almost twenty years earlier.[72] A year earlier, UN troops had arrived in Cyprus – sent as a buffer between battling Greeks and Turks.[73] Those troops, and observers, continue on assignment.

Almost forty years of UN peacekeeping experience highlight several issues. First, peacekeeping has been most effective when *both* sides welcomed the third party and when the latter maintained strict neutrality. The UNEF II force in the Sinai and the UNDOF force on the Golan Heights perhaps best illustrate this. Second, and related to the above, classic border operations are far more likely to succeed than confusing internal 'policing'. Cyprus and the Congo are examples of the latter, where providing a 'buffer' carries a far different meaning than it would on the clearly demarcated Golan Heights. Third, the power of the peacekeeping troops lies not in their weaponry, but in their moral and political force. Sydney Bailey, in his *How Wars End*, argues:

> The international force is not there to impose a solution or even to enforce the cessation of hostilities: its function is partly symbolic, and the safety of UN peacekeeping personnel lies in the brassards [a cloth band with the UN insignia] or blue berets of its members and not in the weapons they carry.[74]

Roy Finch agrees: 'The arms of the UNEF troops in the Near East are only a token; the 2,000-man force could easily be crushed by either side. It is effective only because it is backed up by "world opinion" and by the big powers.'[75] In spite of admitted failures, the UN role has been largely constructive. The superpowers have yet to find a better way.

Reaching for an International Non-violent Peace Guard

The recent story probably begins in 1948. Pacifists worldwide had arranged a meeting with the man everyone viewed as their spiritual leader – Mahatma Gandhi. His assassination, however, forced postponement to December 1949. Out of this World Pacifist Conference came a proposal to form Satyagraha (Gandhi's word for non-violence) Units.[76]

The proposal lay dormant until 1957, when Vinoba Bhave of India implemented one of Gandhi's dreams by creating the 'Shanti Senas' or Peace Brigades.[77] Resolving communal conflict between Muslims and Hindus, including the quelling of raging mobs, was the special mission of this non-violent Peace Brigade. When burning and killing broke out between Hindus and Muslims, the Shanti Senas marched unarmed into the middle of the mobs, protected only by their identifying sash and their record of goodwill in all communities. By 1969, there were thirteen thousand volunteers organised in local, district, state and national levels.

The Shanti Sena also threw themselves into the gramdon movement (a movement designed to create inter-religious communal harmony at the village level). In some fifty thousand gramdon villages, the Shanti Sena were responsible for guarding the village and maintaining peace.[78]

Narayan Desai, later director of the Shanti Senas, led the group during religious riots in Ahmedabad, India. In September 1969 the city erupted in Hindu–Muslim strife. Thousands died in a rampage that devastated much of the urban area. Immediately Shanti Sena volunteers poured into Ahmedabad. They moved fearlessly throughout the city, visiting one riot-affected area after another. The Shanti Sena engaged in arbitration, clean-up, relief efforts and education. After four months of work, the volunteers celebrated success with a procession shouting: 'We may be Hindus, we may be Muslims, but above all, we are human beings.'[79]

In 1960, pacifists from both East and West met in India. Known as the 'Triennial Conference of the War Resisters International', the meeting accelerated a pacifist trend towards international peacekeeping. Two leaders in particular pressed the peacekeeping concept: Jayaprakash Narayan of India and the Spanish republican Salvador de Madariaga. Their proposal envisaged an unarmed 'Peace Guard' serving under UN auspices.[80] In a joint statement, Narayan and de Madariaga asserted:

> The presence of a body of regular World Guards or Peace Guards, intervening with no weapons whatsoever between two forces combatting or about to combat, might have considerable effect. They would not be there as a fanciful improvisation, but as the positive and practical application of a previously negotiated and ratified Additional Charter binding all United Nations members. This Charter should ensure:
>
> (1) Inviolability of the World Guards;
> (2) their right to go anywhere at any time from the day they are given an assignment by the United Nations;
> (3) their right to go and intervene in any conflict of any nature when asked by only one of the parties thereto or by third parties or the Secretary General.
>
> The World Guards would be parachutists. They should be able to stop advancing armies by refusing to move from roads, railways, or airfields. They would be empowered to act in any capacity their chiefs might think adequate for the situation, though they would never use force.[81]

Narayan and de Madariaga sent the statement to Dag Hammerskjöld at the United Nations, but never received any response. The proposal – while bold – remained theoretical.

Pacifists continued their search for concrete structures for non-violent intervention in armed conflict in the 1960s. In 1962, the World Peace Brigade was formed. The founding statement declared that its aim was to '. . . organize, train and keep available a Brigade for non-violent action in situations of potential or actual conflict, internal and international . . . [and] against all war and preparations for war, and the continuing development of weapons of mass destruction'.[82]

The fledgling Brigade did assemble for action in Zambia (then Northern Rhodesia). Kenneth Kaunda had requested that a force of primarily African marchers be ready to move into Northern Rhodesia. Kaunda was concerned that white stalling of the election process might provoke a black backlash. More than five thousand unarmed persons massed on the Northern Rhodesian border in response to Kaunda's call. Though most were Africans, some had come from Europe, Asia and the United States. In the end, the dispute was resolved peacefully and the marchers were not needed.[83]

The Shanti Sena and World Peace Brigade came together in 1962 to form the Delhi-Peking Friendship March in response to the Sino–Indian border clash. The marchers hoped to take their message of non-violence and reconciliation across the miles from Delhi to Peking. Unfortunately, the international group was denied entry by countries bordering India. Yet the march did demonstrate the growing longing for some international peace team capable of non-violent intervention in international conflict.

A Canoe Blockade of American Ports

On 14 July 1971, three kayaks, three canoes, and a
rubber raft blocked the path of a huge Pakistani
freighter steaming in to load arms at the port of Baltimore.[84] The next day the Foreign Affairs Committee of
the US House of Representatives voted to withhold all
military and economic aid from Pakistan. A dramatic
form of non-violent intervention had played its part.

The Bengalis of East Pakistan (now Bangladesh) had
chafed under the domination of West Pakistan. Then, in
December 1970, the Awami League, which championed
greater autonomy for East Pakistan, won a clear electoral victory. In response, the Pakistani dictator unleashed his army on East Pakistan on 25 March 1971.
By the time the war ended, a million Bengalis had been
killed, twenty-five thousand women had been raped,
and nine million refugees had fled to India.[85]

As the Pakistani army continued to rampage through
Bengal, the US government denied that it was aiding
Pakistan. But it was. The US was shipping large
amounts of war material to Pakistan from East-coast
American ports.

In *Blockade*, an exciting book that reads like a first-
rate novel, Richard Taylor describes the daring adven-
ture of the 'non-violent fleet' which helped stop this flow
of arms. Taylor and other Philadelphia Quakers decided to dramatise the US shipment of arms by paddling
their canoes in front of the steamship *Padma* as it came
into the Baltimore harbour. Obviously their lives were
at risk. As it turned out, they were plucked out of the
water by the US coastguard, which then escorted the
Padma to dock. But the news coverage of their action
contributed to the vote by the House Foreign Affairs
Committee the next day. And the next week the block-

aders flew to Miami and persuaded the US Longshoremen not to load any more arms destined for Pakistan.

The action then moved to Philadelphia. More canoes
blockaded another Pakistani ship, the *Al Ahmadi*, as
the Longshoremen watched. The blockaders' daring
persuaded the dock workers to refuse to load the ship,
thus shutting the port of Philadelphia to all Pakistani
ships, regardless of their cargo.

Finally, in early November, the Nixon Administration ended all shipment of arms to Pakistan. Obviously
many factors led to that decision. But the activity of the
'non-violent fleet' clearly played a part.

Peace Brigades International

The groping for an international non-violent peace
guard begun in the Thirties, and continued in the
Fifties and Sixties, reached a new level of implementation and success in the 1980s with Peace Brigades
International and Witness for Peace. (The latter story
will have to wait for the next chapter.)

'Peace Brigades International' (PBI) was born at an
international consultation in Canada in September
1981. PBI is clearly based on the foundation of Gandhi,
Shanti Sena and the disbanded World Peace Brigade,
and the success of Martin Luther King's non-violent
civil rights crusade. Its founding statement reads in
part:

> We are forming an organization with the capability to
> mobilize and provide trained units of volunteers. These
> units may be assigned to areas of high tension to avert
> violent outbreaks. If hostile clashes occur, a brigade may
> establish and monitor a cease-fire, offer mediatory ser-
> vices, or carry on works of reconstruction and reconcili-
> ation . . . We are building on a rich and extensive heritage
> of nonviolent action, which can no longer be ignored.[86]

PBI is more than a philosophical statement. Its members have seen 'action' on the Nicaraguan border and within the troubled borders of Guatemala.[87]

PBI's most successful action has been its non-violent 'escort duty' for endangered mothers in Guatemala. Members of PBI accompany threatened leaders of GAM (Grupo de apoyo mutuo) twenty-four hours a day.

GAM is a group of parents (largely mothers), formed in June 1984 to protest the disappearance of their children.[88] In Guatemala, right-wing death squads frequently kidnap, torture and kill anyone involved in improving the lot of the poor. Very few of GAM's members have had any previous political involvement. But the pain of their disappeared children prompted them to place newspaper advertisements, hold regular vigils and petition the government with one simple question: 'Where are our loved ones?'

For a year, GAM was tolerated. But in March 1985, General Victores, the Chief of State, charged (falsely) that 'forces of subversion' were manipulating GAM. A barrage of anonymous death threats followed. Within a few weeks two key leaders of GAM had been murdered. One of these, Hector Gomez, was found with his head bashed in and his tongue cut out.

PBI offered to supply international, round-the-clock escorts to accompany the other leaders of GAM. Since these international escorts from PBI arrived in May 1985, no board member of GAM has been kidnapped or harmed. The task is nerve-racking. One never knows when a bullet or bomb might kill escort or friend. The work is so emotionally draining that escorts must rotate out every few weeks. But it works.

PBI has expanded its activities. It has provided a non-violent watch at the site of a labour union strike. A team went to El Salvador at the invitation of a

Lutheran bishop. PBI is also providing staff to help
develop the New World Centre for Nonviolent Resolution of Conflict based in Bogota, Columbia under the
auspices of the United Nations University for Peace.
Conversations have begun exploring escort services for
Salvadoran human rights organisations. And there are
explorations with people in Sri Lanka and South
Africa.[89] PBI's success in Guatemala brings the vision
of an effective, non-violent international peace guard
one small important step closer to fruition.

This chapter has skipped quickly over a long history
of daring experimentation with alternatives to war.
We explored only a few of the stories of non-violent
resistance.

We could have looked at John Adams' insistence,
after his extremely dangerous non-violent struggle to
contain the fighting at Wounded Knee (1973), that 'at
times a person has to fight for non-violence'.[90] We could
have examined the Alagamar Land Struggle in Brazil
(late 1970s) and Archbishop Dom Helder Camara's
chasing of the landlord's cattle off the peasants' fields.[91]
We might have noted the massacre that never occurred
in Rio de Janeiro in 1968 because 'a dozen priests
offered themselves as the first victims'.[92] We could
have explored the Philadelphia Quakers' non-violent
police force at the Black Panther's Convention in
1970.[93]

Because it is so well known, I hardly mentioned
Martin Luther King, Jr's extremely important non-
violent civil rights crusade which substantially
changed American society.[94] In any comprehensive sur-
vey of the emergence of non-violent alternatives, King
would deserve many chapters. In this short sketch we
can only acknowledge with gratitude that, other than
Gandhi, his vision and leadership have done more than

anyone else's to make non-violent action a thinkable alternative to violence for millions of people.

That non-violent direct action exists is beyond dispute. That it often succeeds is an irrefutable part of the historical record. That it, therefore, attracts growing interest in the late twentieth century is hardly surprising.

That increasing attention is due in part to some very recent successes. Non-violent action has, in the last few years, helped to neutralise a guerrilla army dear to the heart of Ronald Reagan and overthrow a dictator as tough as Ferdinand Marcos of the Philippines. To those stories of peaceful daring we turn in the next two chapters.

2　NON-VIOLENT INTERVENTION IN GUERRILLA WARFARE

You take risks for peace just as you take risks for war.
Sharon Hostetler[1]

I was scared on the morning of 11 January 1985. Along with about twenty other Witness for Peace volunteers, I was riding a dusty bus down a twisting road in a remote guerrilla-infested part of Northern Nicaragua. As we wound our way down the hillside into the valley towards the small town of San Juan de Limay, we knew a thousand US-funded contras lay hidden in the surrounding hills.

The contras had announced their intention to capture the encircled town. Frequent ambushes and attacks on surrounding villages, farm houses and cooperatives had occurred. Nancy Donovan, an American Maryknoll sister from the town, had been kidnapped and then released three days earlier. In the previous month, the contras had captured and tortured many civilians. Thirty-three had died. The contras' attacks had closed all roads to the town for a month.

Our bus was the first outside vehicle to try to break that blockade. As we slowly navigated the twisting roads down the side of the hills and then drove past burnt tractors destroyed by the contras, I prayed hard that there would be no sudden burst of gunfire, no surprise ambush. There wasn't. We arrived safely in the town. (It would be bad politics to use US-supplied weapons to kill American Christians.)

I was relieved, and the townsfolk were overjoyed. Later we were told that the people of San Juan de Limay slept more securely that night than they had in weeks. They knew an attack was very unlikely while American Christians were present.[2]

My little personal pilgrimage of fear and faith is one tiny part of a much larger story. Coming in teams of about twenty each, 2300 Americans have travelled to Nicaragua with Witness for Peace.[3] One team rode a rusty fishing boat to rendezvous with a huge US warship. Eden Pastora's contras kidnapped another team while they were sailing up the Rio San Juan that flows between Nicaragua and Costa Rica. Others faced more mundane hardships – like coping with upset digestive sytems that demanded hasty, frequent treks to unfamiliar toilets.

What has prompted so many comfortable American Christians to risk disease, injury and even death in a non-violent challenge to the guerrillas invading Nicaragua?

A History of Outside Intervention

The story begins early in this century.[4] As the noted Cornell University historian Walter LaFeber has pointed out in a recent scholarly study,

> Modern Nicaragua . . . was shaped by U.S. military occupation (1911–33), and then the U.S. created and supported Somoza family dynasty (1934–79). That family seized most of the wealth, including land area equal to the size of Massachusetts. Meanwhile 200,000 peasants had no land. The major causes of death were gastrointestinal and parasitic diseases, and infant maladies.[5]

Illiteracy was about sixty percent. The majority of Nicaraguans prior to the 1979 revolution faced appalling living conditions. Although Americans were obviously not responsible for a great deal of the poverty and agony, there was a connection between US policy and the conditions in Nicaragua. 'Dependency' is the word LaFeber uses to describe the relationship of Nicaragua (and Central America generally) to the US. It is a dependency that ties Central American economies to a few export crops sold to the US and leads to wealth for a ruling élite and poverty and malnutrition for the rest. Furthermore, as demonstrated in the cases of Nicaragua and Guatemala, when 'economic leverage proved incapable of reversing trends that North American officials despised and feared', the US 'intervened frequently with troops or covert operations to ensure that ties of dependence remained'.[6]

On 19 July 1979, at the cost of perhaps as many as fifty thousand lives, a broad coalition of Nicaraguan people joined in a popular insurrection to overthrow the corrupt Somoza dictatorship. To the bitter end, some powerful US interests continued to support the brutal dictator. As late as 22 June 1979, Secretary of State Cyrus Vance called on the OAS to send a 'peacekeeping force' to Somoza's aid. Some days earlier, 130 US congressmen had demanded the restoration of direct military aid to the dictator. The liberal alternatives to Somoza and the guerrillas within Nicaragua could not compete with the powerful 'Somoza lobby' in Washington. Thus the final victory was directed and led by the leftist guerrilla movement, the Sandinista Front for National Liberation (FSLN). On 19 July, Nicaragua embarked on its socialist political venture, vowing to redistribute the land among the people, educate and provide health care for the masses, and establish a mixed economy to be run, it was claimed, in the interests of Nicaraguans rather than foreign investors.

Regardless of how one views the ruling Sandinista government of Nicaragua (and I give it a very mixed review),[7] it is undeniable that the Nicaraguan revolution brought immediate benefits to the poorest segments of the population. There was new hope for a brighter future for the many poor and disadvantaged. Anthony Quainton, the US ambassador to Nicaragua in the earlier years of the Reagan administration, admitted on a number of occasions that the Sandinista government had in fact brought about significant improvement in land distribution, health, nutrition, and education for the Nicaraguan population as a whole.[8]

From the beginning, the Reagan administration was bitterly opposed to the Sandinista government. And there were reasons for concern. The anti-American rhetoric had already prompted the Carter administration to withhold some aid. Promised elections were not held for five years, and there were Marxist-Leninists in the Sandinista coalition along with nationalists and Catholics. Actions designed to undercut the independence of other centres of power such as independent trade unions occurred. All these were valid reasons for anxiety. But they hardly justified the simplistic charge that the Sandinista party was a monolithic Marxist-Leninist group determined to destroy the church and impose a Soviet-style totalitarian society. Undoubtedly some Sandinista members wanted that. Others did not.

Instead of following a balanced policy of protesting violations of human rights and democratic freedoms, the US government launched its secret war in late 1981. The US trained and financed a counter-revolutionary movement (called the contras) led by former officers of Somoza's private army. The stated aim of this 'covert' operation was to stop the flow of arms from Nicaragua to El Salvador and to 'destabilise' the Sandinista government. Later, however, when the contra army numbered over ten thousand fighters and the US offered no convincing evidence of substantial arms flow to El Salvador, the administration admitted that it had embarked on an effort to 'overthrow' the Sandinista government and to make it 'say Uncle'.[9]

The result has been enormous suffering and massacre in Nicaragua. In its brief to the World Court, Nicaragua claimed that contra violence had killed 2600 persons; maimed, raped or kidnapped 5500; and displaced 150,000 civilians.[10]

Many independent reporters and eyewitnesses have recounted widespread attacks on civilians. Contrary to the just war tradition's prohibition against targetting civilians, the contras almost daily kidnap, torture, mutilate and kill non-combatants. During my trip to San Juan de Limay in January1985, I listened to the local medical doctor describe how the contras had broken fingers, mutilated and dismembered the bodies of the thirty-three people they had killed the previous month near that one small town. The son of the woman who was to be our cook was so badly tortured and mutilated that his father could identify him only because of his belt.[11] Independent human rights organisations like America's Watch and Amnesty International have consistently reported similar contra atrocities against civilians.[12]

Many American citizens were outraged at the expenditure of their tax dollars to support this carnage.

Witness for Peace Begins

In July 1983, an interdenominational group of 150 US citizens took a dramatic new step of non-violent intervention in guerrilla warfare. They travelled to the Nicaraguan–Honduran border to be present with the people suffering attacks and to pray and keep vigil for peace. While present in the beleaguered border town of Jalapa, the delegation witnessed the terrible effects of the war on the population. They also brought hope and temporary safety. One grateful Jalapa resident told the group, 'At least tonight they won't shell us, because you are here.'[13]

An idea began to germinate among the vigilers. If their mere presence could provide security from attacks by the contras, why not establish a 'permanent presence' of US citizens to stand non-violently with the Nicaraguan people?

Before the group left Nicaragua, plans emerged for a permanent presence in Nicaragua, originally envisaged as numbering hundreds of volunteers stationed along the border. Two religious groups within Nicaragua issued a formal invitation and agreed to act as sponsors: The Evangelical Committee for Aid and Development (CEPAD), an evangelical Protestant development agency representing thirty-seven evangelical denominations, and the Antonio Valdivieso Ecumenical Center, an agency promoting religious and social research. Unfortunately, the government of Honduras rejected a request to operate there too. But the Nicaraguan government gave preliminary approval, including the important provision that the project would be politically non-aligned and would support no party in Nicaragua.

The new organisation was called Witness for Peace

(WFP). Its history is a story of transition from Spirit-inspired dream to dusty reality. The first four volunteers left the US for Nicaragua in October 1983. The earliest focus of WFP was the town of Jalapa in Northern Nicaragua. (At that time the contras hoped to capture the town, establish a provisional government, and seek 'aid' from 'friendly countries'.) WFP's initial 'modest' goal was to establish a team of ten to twenty 'permanent' witnesses who would commit themselves to a six-month stay at the Nicaraguan border. Periodically, 'Short Term Teams', staying in Nicaragua for only one or two weeks, would join them. It was hoped that the permanent presence along the border would number at least fifty at all times – a far cry from several hundred, but in itself a considerable undertaking!

In December 1983, the first Short Term Team arrived for a two-week stay. From the start the visits of the Short Term Teams were conceived as 'educational' opportunities at the same time as they were oppor tunities to promote peace in the war zones. The two weeks spent in Nicaragua included interviews with both opponents and supporters of the Sandinista revolution.

As 1984 unfolded, the organisation grew both in Nicaragua and in the US. Eventually a 'manageable' operation emerged, comprising a Steering Committee, a small full-time staff, plus many volunteers in the US and Nicaragua. At the heart of the operation was a 'long-term' team of between fifteen to twenty permanent volunteers in Nicaragua, and three delegations of Short Term volunteers visiting Nicaragua every month. That basic pattern was to continue for the next three years. By early 1987, 2300 WFP volunteers had visited Nicaragua.

Goals and Strategy

WFP's fundamental goal was to end the US-funded guerrilla warfare in Nicaragua. The method was non-violent direct action. WFP's official statement of purpose pledges 'to plumb the depths of the religious nonviolent tradition and continually to envision and experiment with creative, powerful nonviolent actions'. Boldly they declared themselves ready 'to take risks in the struggle for peace comparable to the risks people take in war'.[14]

The initial strategy in Jalapa was 'deterrence through interpositioning'. The contras planned to seize the town. WFP therefore hoped that by placing themselves in the town they could deter the contras, who, for political reasons, would find it costly to wound or kill American citizens.

This strategy, however, worked only for a short time because contra strategy soon changed. Aborting their effort to seize a major town, the contras began attacking isolated farms, cooperatives, and government-funded projects like schools and clinics in order to destroy the social and economic infrastructure of the country. They targetted key civilian workers and community leaders (especially teachers, doctors and agricultural specialists) for abduction, torture and assassination. It was totally unthinkable for a few dozen WFP volunteers to try to stand between even a tiny fraction of the Nicaraguan people and ten thousand guerrillas engaged in hit-and-run terrorist attacks on constantly shifting targets across Northern Nicaragua. Interpositioning, however, was not entirely abandoned. It happened dramatically in the case of the encounter with the US warship. Arnold Snyder, who led WFP's Nicaraguan team for a year, thinks it would have worked in San Juan de Limay in late 1984 and early 1985 if there had been enough volunteers.[15] Overall, however, deterrence through interpositioning does not fit the tactics of guerrilla warfare.

WFP therefore redirected its efforts towards visiting places recently attacked in order to document and publicise the targetting of civilians. The contra attack on exclusively civilian and economic targets in the town of Octal on 1 June 1984 helped shape this redirection. In their assault, the contras ignored the army base in Octal. Instead, they destroyed the country's largest lumber mill, offices of the electric company, grain storage silos, and many other vital economic plants and facilities. WFP volunteers arrived the next day to help with clean-up and reconstruction, and to publicise the atrocities. One WFP volunteer discovered a CIA-written manual designed to teach Nicaraguans how to destabilise and sabotage their government and economy.[16] Publicising the evidence of this CIA manual helped galvanise American public opinion against funding the contras.

Since 1984, in fact, the central strategy of WFP has been to mobilise public opinion to change US policy by documenting and publicising the ravaging of the civilian population. WFP publishes frequent 'Newsbriefs' based on eyewitness testimony gathered by WFP volunteers, and a bimonthly *Witness for Peace Newsletter* (with a circulation of twenty-five thousand). A regularly updated telephone 'Hotline' in the US provides a steady flow of direct information from WFP staff in Managua. Every month, three teams of short-term volunteers return to the US to speak to churches and write or stimulate articles for church and secular media. WFP has also given testimony to the US Congress. Coverage has reached a hundred million

Americans.[17] That is substantial, and has undoubtedly made a difference.

Admittedly, the coverage has been spotty and sporadic in the major news media. Unfortunately mainline US media are excessively concerned with news that sells newspapers and raises TV ratings in the US itself. Therefore the kidnapping of an American nun or the encounter of a shrimp boat full of US citizens with a US Navy frigate makes headlines. Daily mutilation and assassinations of Nicaraguan civilians do not. But even within these limitations, WFP has generated significant media coverage. As a result, its non-violent action in Nicaragua has played a crucial role in arousing US public opinion against the war.

Not surprisingly WFP's two most dramatic episodes — the encounter with a US warship, and the kidnapping along the San Juan river — attracted the most attention.

Challenging a US Warship

On 6 November 1984, President Ronald Reagan won a second term as President in a landslide victory at the polls. That same evening his government announced that US warships were tracking a Soviet freighter bound for Nicaragua's Corinto harbour. On board, it was claimed, were crates similar to those used to transport Soviet MiG fighters. Fear of war skyrocketed as the US government implied that it would never tolerate the alleged Soviet MiGs, which would 'upset the delicate balance of power in the region'.

On 7 November the Soviet freighter bearing the mysterious crates approached the Nicaraguan harbour of Corinto. It was already within Nicaraguan territorial waters, just seven miles from the coast, when two US

Navy frigates gave chase. When a Nicaraguan coast-guard cutter went to meet the Soviet ship, it was then pursued by one of the frigates, which came within five miles of the coast. An unmarked C-130 aircraft overflew the port, drawing anti-aircraft fire from onshore batteries. Fears of invasion mounted even though the Nicaraguan government repeatedly denied the presence of MiG fighter aircraft on the Soviet freighter. The government of Nicaragua called the country to mobilise for defence. The government announced that student production brigades, in all numbering twenty thousand young people, would abandon their project of picking coffee and cotton, and mobilise instead for the defence of Managua. Managua would be sold 'barrio by barrio'* if the US decided to invade. In the international arena, Nicaragua called for an emergency meeting of the United Nations Security Council. In Nicaraguan cities, people hurriedly began digging community air raid shelters and neighbourhood militia were issued arms.

It was in this charged atmosphere that twelve long-term volunteers in WFP gathered together in Managua on 8 November to share a noon meal, reflect on Scripture, pray, and plan. Their feelings are best expressed by Arnold Snyder, who was then Nicaraguan Coordinator of WFP:

> We shared a feeling that an evil force beyond all human control was propelling events toward a terrible and bloody conclusion. The time of sharing and prayer drew us together and strengthened us; the presence of the Holy Spirit was unmistakable in the coming of hope and the banishing of fear. We were moved from helplessness to a time of planning for action, trying to conceive of ways in which we could most effectively stand up to be counted as opposing the further violence our government seemed bent on imposing on the people of Nicaragua.

* A barrio is a poor community or district.

The most outlandish idea to surface was also the most inspired: that we rent a flotilla of boats and place ourselves between the US frigates and town and harbor of Corinto.[18]

'Wetness for Peace', as it was quickly dubbed, demanded speed. Two WFP Short Term delegations in different parts of Nicaragua had to be assembled. They needed government permission to enter the war zone. They rushed to notify the press, assemble food, transportation and rent a boat – all in one and a half days.

At noon on Saturday, eighty US citizens, accompanied by twenty international journalists, converged on Corinto. But their 'peace flotilla' was modest in the extreme. One rusty old shrimp boat, the *Subtiava*, would sail forth to challenge the US Navy frigate with a message of peace.

Arnold Snyder's words capture the mood of the non-violent marines:

> Those of us gathered for worship in the Baptist church of Corinto continued to feel the dark threat of war around us, but there was also an unmistakable presence of God's peace in the midst of the storm, expressed by the songs that began spontaneously as we waited for the service to begin. As we have so often had to note in our work in Witness for Peace, God strengthens us in special and unexpected ways when we leave our private fears and join together in common purpose.[19]

Following a moving service and prayer of commissioning, they marched through the town to the boat, carrying banners and singing songs of hope and victory. Forty people clambered aboard and the trusty *Subtiava* pulled away from the dock in a cloud of diesel smoke. Slowly it moved towards international waters and an uncertain encounter. Those left on shore prayed together in the ruins of the fuel storage tanks destroyed by the CIA attack on Corinto in October 1983.

After two hours, a small dot appeared on the horizon. As the third hour passed, the forbidding outline of a US warship loomed ever larger. As the sun began to sink over the horizon, the little shrimp boat sailed within a kilometre of the huge ship, awesome with its constantly moving radar antennae and its artillery and missile batteries now visible. Just as the *Subtiava* came within hailing distance, the warship began to move. The little shrimper increased its speed to close the distance, but the warship suddenly turned towards the open sea and sped away.

As the Navy ship began to move away, the Rev. Stuart Taylor of the Long Term Team grabbed a loud-speaker and shouted to the US sailors on the departing warship, 'Why are you here? Why are you threatening the people of Nicaragua? Go away! Leave us and these people in peace!' But by this time the great ship was well out of earshot and turning towards open sea. David had come to speak to Goliath without so much as a sling in hand, but the giant would have none of it.

The non-violent marines in the tiny shrimp boat were disappointed. They had hoped to speak to the American sailors on board the ship, but not a single person on the frigate was visible the entire time. The final appeal had to be directed towards a huge mute machine.

But the rendezvous was a success even though the message of peace was not communicated directly to the crew of the warship. It was filmed, recorded, and reported to millions around the world from the United States and Canada to Europe, Latin America, Africa and Asia. The image of the great warship retreating from the unarmed, rusty tub conveyed its own message. At the farewell service on Thanksgiving Day, after many days of maintaining a permanent vigil on the beach of Corinto, Baptist pastor Ernesto Cordova reminded the WFP volunteers: 'The little ship did not have fire power, but it had the power of love, the power of justice, the power of God. And the weakness of God is stronger than the power of men.' One courageous act of non-violent interpositioning had played its small part in nudging leaders and national public opinion away from violent conflict. By Thanksgiving, the threats of attack and fears of invasion subsided.

Kidnapped by the Contras

Twenty-one months later, WFP volunteers again captured news headlines around the world. Travelling down the Rio San Juan in the first non-military vessel to travel on the river beyond El Castillo for over two years, fifty-six people with WFP were kidnapped by the contras.[20]

In the preceding months, tensions had risen along the Rio San Juan which flows between Costa Rica and Nicaragua. The contras were launching regular raids into Nicaragua and then retreating to the Costa Rican side. On 31 May 1985, someone killed two Costa Rican Civil Guards near the river inside Costa Rica. The Sandinistas blamed the contras and the contras blamed the Sandinistas. Many feared some new incident could provide a pretext for US intervention.

WFP decided to sail a 'peace flotilla' down the dangerous section of the river. A delegation of twenty-nine WFP volunteers and sixteen members of the press was ready to embark on 6 August 1935.

The day before, however, Eden Pastora, leader of the contras operating from Costa Rica, issued a press release announcing that he had ordered his men to fire on 'wolves in sheep's clothing'. At their press conference,

WFP responded with firmness: 'For centuries, Christian theologians have justified the risking of human life to wage war. In Nicaragua today, we are called to take risks for peace.'[21] Later, Sharon Hostetler, joint coordinator of WFP in Nicaragua, said during an interview with CBS: 'We hope to God, like all the Nicaraguans, that none of us will be killed. We are willing to risk danger . . . But we pray and reflect on the fact that the call to peace is not easy. You take risks for peace just as you take risks for war.'[22]

Flying a large WFP banner, the delegation sailed from El Castillo on 6 August. The journey downstream was peaceful. But the next morning, on the return voyage, trouble unexpectedly erupted. Shots rang across the bows and everyone hit the deck. Guerrillas ordered the boat to the Costa Rican shore and identified themselves as members of ARDE (Pastora's contra organisation).

The next thirty hours were terrifying. At the command of their armed kidnappers, everyone, including an elderly woman and an eighty year old man in the delegation, stumbled uphill through difficult jungle terrain. Sandals fell off in deep mud. Too exhausted to trudge further, they were finally allowed to rest in a thatched hut one and a half miles from the river.

Towards evening, the guerrillas decided to let the group return to the boat. People slipped and fell on the muddy downhill path, rendered more treacherous by the all-day rain. They got lost and separated from each other, finally reaching the boat only after dark. But William, the guerrilla leader, was furious, partly because of embarrassment at losing his way. Enraged, he ordered them to march up the hill to the hut again in the darkness.

The old woman collapsed on the ground, sobbing. Her

feet were bleeding. Totally exhausted, she had no energy to obey the orders and march another one and a half miles. That was the most terrifying moment of the entire episode. Many feared they would shoot the old woman. She feared others would die because of her.

Eventually William grudgingly agreed to allow everyone on board for the night, provided they kept the lights out and made no noise. Finally, in the early afternoon of the next day, they were all released. With song and prayer, they gratefully reboarded their boat and finished the return voyage.

No peace treaties were signed because of the short voyage of this peace flotilla. But radio, television and newspapers around the world broadcast a new chapter in the amazing story of non-violent resistance.

Evaluating Witness for Peace

Has WFP been successful? The war has not ended. The Sandinista government continues to commit human rights violations. The contras continue to murder civilians. And the American taxpayers continue to fund the carnage.

That was the state of affairs at the end of 1987. Then the unexpected happened in 1988. The US Congress ended funding for lethal weapons for the contras, and the Sandinistas and contras sat down to negotiate an end to the war. As this book goes to press, it is impossible to say how those negotiations – which look very hopeful at present – will finally end.

There is no doubt, however, that Witness for Peace has played a significant role in the complicated history of US–Nicaraguan relations during the Reagan era.

Occasionally, the presence of WFP has deterred attack. Documentation and publication of civilian casualties has influenced US policy. And WFP has forged another courageous model of non-violent direct action.

Deterrence of contra attack has been very modest, but not irrelevant. The presence (and publicity about the presence) of WFP in Jalapa was probably *one* factor in the contra's abandoning that objective in 1983. The contras did not attack San Juan de Limay while my delegation was there. The US warship clearly did not want to deal with a shrimp boat full of praying American Christians accompanied by international journalists.

Because of intercepted radio messages describing WFP vehicles and activities, WFP knows that the contras are informed about WFP activities and report on their movements. Only one town has been attacked while WFP volunteers were present.

Had they wished to do so, the contras could easily have ambushed WFP delegates many times as they drove the isolated roads in the war zones. Since the contras clearly do not wish to kill US citizens, this translates into a measure of protection for the Nicaraguan people while WFP volunteers are present. A highly placed Nicaraguan government official, when asked if WFP's non-violent presence deterred attack, answered unequivocally, 'Yes, it helps. Because the one thing that is feared by the Reagan government is that U.S. citizens might die ... So yes, it matters that non-violent Christians are present as a barrier.'[23]

Gilberto Aguirre, Executive Director of CEPAD, the evangelical agency in Nicaragua that has worked closely with WFP, has said the same thing: 'You have to extend and increase Witness for Peace work. We have seen that the impact of your work is very great, not only in the U.S.A. but with the contras. You could save a lot of lives.'[24]

On balance, however, one must conclude that the deterrent effect of WFP has at best been only a modest nuisance for the contras.

More important than WFP's attempt at deterrence has been its growing impact on US public opinion and indirectly on US public policy through the documentation and publication of civilian casualties. The aim is to change a policy, not simply to be willing to risk death by interpositioning oneself between warring factions. If no one is willing to take such a risk, of course, there will be nothing to tell. But if they do, the story must then be told.

And it has been. WFP estimates that fifty-one million people have heard over a thousand radio and TV interviews of returning delegations. Fifty-three million people have read over a thousand feature stories, interviews and leader columns. Nine million people have read over 650 articles in church publications. Four hundred thousand individuals have heard over eight thousand in-person presentations to local church and community groups. Over sixty million Americans saw or read national media coverage of the kidnapped delegation on the Rio San Juan. Probably a hundred million Americans in all have been reached.[25]

Reaching that many Americans even very infrequently has undoubtedly helped shape US public opinion. WFP deserves some of the credit for the fact that a majority of Americans oppose US support for the contras and persuaded the US Congress to deny funding to them from 1984 to 1986 and again in 1988. That one of the most popular presidents in American history has been unable to rally majority support for his top foreign policy objective is due in part to WFP.

Finally, WFP is having an intangible but important long-term impact. Even its modest success has opened the eyes of untold thousands to a non-violent alternative for resisting violence. The influence of thousands of returning volunteers excited about the potential of non-violent direct action is working its way through American churches like yeast in dough. Nor is the impact limited to the US. News of this effort has spread to many countries. Perhaps the comment of a (non-pacifist) Baptist leader in Nicaragua typifies the educational impact of WFP in many places: 'I didn't understand non-violence at first. I came to understand non-violent action for peace by the testimony of the witnesses [WFP volunteers] in a place where the people were being violated by force of arms.'[26]

WFP is one subplot in a living, growing story of courageous pioneers seeking alternatives to lethal violence.[27] WFP's part of that developing story demonstrates that non-violent resistance to guerrilla warfare is possible.[28] The Philippine People's Revolution, to which we turn in the next chapter, shows that non-violent revolution is also realistic.

3   WHEELCHAIRS vs TANKS

> I have decided to pursue my freedom struggle
> through the path of nonviolence . . . I refuse to believe
> that it is necessary for a nation to build its foundation
> on the bones of its youth.
>
> Benigno Aquino[1]

The most stunning non-violent victory since Mahatma
Gandhi and Martin Luther King occurred in the Philippines in early 1986. Praying nuns, nursing mothers and
old women in wheelchairs turned back bayonets and
tanks. In four breathtaking days in late February,
Filipino 'people power' toppled President Ferdinand
Marcos, one of the world's most durable dictators.

Marcos and his Opponents

The story of course began much earlier. Marcos won the
presidential election in 1965. In 1972, he declared
martial law, which was not lifted until 1981. Even
then, extra-legal powers enabled him to continue his
repressive role.

Marcos used dictatorial powers to amass great wealth
for himself, close friends, and cooperative foreign com-
panies.[2] To promote his development policy based on
export crops, he ruthlessly suppressed workers who
demanded decent wages and land reform. (Towards the
end of his rule, the average wage for a sugar-cane cutter

working thirteen to fourteen hours a day was $7.00 a week.) Both Amnesty International and the International Commission of Jurists documented thousands of political prisoners in Marcos' jails. Electric shock torture, water torture, extended solitary confinement and beatings were common. Such measures propped up a system where a tiny portion of the population received a huge percent of the nation's total personal income.[3]

While Marcos and company stashed billions in Swiss banks, the majority of the people suffered grinding poverty. Three quarters of the people lived below the poverty line. Seventy-seven percent of all children under six suffered from malnutrition.

Not surprisingly, a Marxist guerrilla movement gained increasing acceptance. A tiny group when Marcos declared martial law in 1972, the Marxist-led New People's Army had grown into a strong national movement by the mid 1980s. Many prominent people felt civil war was inevitable. It might take ten years of bloody battle, they guessed, but no other course seemed viable.

But the assassination of Senator Benigno Aquino on 21 August 1983 ignited a fire that brought revolution by different methods.[4] Aquino held the double honour of being Marcos' most prominent political opponent and longest-held (1972–1980) political prisoner. Reading Jesus and Gandhi in prison, this conventional, self-serving politician experienced a renewal of personal faith and a transforming commitment to the poor and non-violence.[5]

Released in 1980 to obtain heart surgery in the US, Aquino prepared himself for the right moment to return home to challenge Marcos' repressive dictatorship. The non-violent tactics he intended to use were abundantly clear in a statement made to the subcommittee on Asian and Pacific Affairs of the US House of Representatives on 23 June 1983:

> To gather empirical data and firsthand information, I travelled to the Middle East, Southeast Asia, and to Central America. I interviewed the leaders of the most 'successful revolutions' and talked to both the victors and the vanquished, the relatives of the victims and the survivors. I have concluded that revolution and violence exact the highest price in terms of human values and human lives in the struggle for freedom. In the end there are really no victors, only victims ...
>
> I have decided to pursue my freedom struggle through the path of nonviolence, fully cognizant that this may be the longer and more arduous road ...
>
> I have chosen to return to the silence of my solitary confinement and from there to work for a peaceful solution to our problems rather than go back triumphant to the blare of trumpets and cymbals seeking to drown the wailing and sad lamentations of mothers whose sons and daughters have been sacrificed to the gods of violent revolution. Can the killers of today be the leaders of tomorrow? Must we destroy in order to build? I refuse to believe that it is necessary for a nation to build its foundation on the bones of its youth.[6]

But Aquino was not to return to his prison cell when he stepped off the plane at Manila International Airport on 21 August 1983. Instead, he dropped dead in a hail of bullets in an assassination almost certainly approved by President Marcos.

The Beginnings of Non-violent Opposition

The country erupted in outrage. Spontaneously, the first major non-violent demonstration in the Philippines occurred. Day and night, millions moved past his coffin in grief and silent defiance. Two million people

marched peacefully in an eleven-hour funeral procession that persisted through sunshine and rain, thunder
and lightning.[7] And they responded enthusiastically
when Aquino's mother and widow begged them to continue the struggle non-violently.

But this emotional outpouring did not immediately
alter political reality. Marcos was still the dictator.
The growing Marxist guerrilla movement (NPA) increasingly appeared to many as the only alternative as
Marcos continued to crack down on opponents.

To be sure, there were a few courageous voices promoting a non-violent alternative. As early as the sixties, some poor communities organised non-violent
struggles and won small but significant victories. Since
the early 1970s, Francisco Claver, bishop on the desper-
ately poor, guerrilla-infested island of Mindanao, had
been promoting non-violent liberation of the poor. Marcos' army called him a Marxist. The Marxist guerrillas
claimed he supported the army. Bishop Claver quietly
continued forming Base Christian Communities committed to a non-violent search for justice in his diocese.
He also promoted the study of non-violent social change
among a small circle of Catholic bishops.[8]

Then in February 1984, a short visit by two veteran
non-violent trainers crystallised more widespread interest in non-violent alternatives. Hildegard and Jean
Goss-Mayr had worked for decades promoting non-
violence in Europe and Latin America. Both
Archbishop Dom Helder Camara of Brazil and the
Nobel Prize winner Adolfo Perez Esquivel of Argentina
have traced their commitment to non-violence to personal encounters with the Goss-Mayrs.[9] As they
travelled through the Philippines in February 1984,
they concluded that the hour was late for any non-
violent effort. But they also sensed a widespread yearn-

ing for some realistic alternative to the agony of civil war.

On the last day of their visit, Butz Aquino (brother of the assassinated Benigno Aquino) met privately with them. Butz Aquino was an active leader in the ongoing protests against the dictatorship. Privately with the Goss-Mayrs, he confided his personal wrestling with the option of armed revolution:

> A few days ago the arms merchants visited us and said to us, 'Do you think that with a few demonstrations you will be able to overthrow this regime? Don't you think you need better weapons than that? We offer them to you. Make up your mind.' ... You see it is providential that you have come just at this point of time, because ever since this visit I am unable to sleep. Do I have the right to throw our country into major civil war? What is my responsibility as a Christian politician in this situation? Is there really such a thing as nonviolent combat against an unjust system like that of Marcos?[10]

In response the Goss-Mayrs challenged him to decide for himself. But they warned that vigorous preparation for non-violent resistance is essential: 'Nonviolence is not something you do spontaneously and without preparation.'[11] They volunteered to return to do seminars if invited.

The invitation came within weeks. In the summer of 1984, the Goss-Mayrs returned for six weeks of seminars on non-violence. They ran seminars for leaders among the political opposition (including Butz Aquino), labour unions, peasants, students, and the church. Bishop Claver organised a three-day seminar for twenty Catholic bishops. Everywhere, the Goss-Mayrs advocated a twofold non-violence: non-violent opposition to the structural violence in Marcos' economic and political system, and abandonment of the inner violence in one's own heart.

The seed of the violence was in the structures, of course, and in the dictator. But wasn't it also in ourselves? It's very easy to say that Marcos is the evil. But unless we each tear the dictator out of our own heart, nothing will change. Another group will come into power and will act similarly to those whom they replaced. So we discovered Marcos within ourselves.[12]

AKKAPKA, a new Philippine organisation committed to non-violence, emerged from these seminars. AKKAPKA (formed in July 1984) is the acronym for Movement for Peace and Justice. It also means 'I embrace you' in Tagalog, the national language of the Philippines. Led by Father Jose Blanco, SJ, AKKAPKA held forty seminars on non-violent social change in thirty different provinces all over the country in its first year.[13]

The numbers seriously interested in using non-violent methods grew rapidly in late 1984 and 1985. Three weeks of seminars in Protestant circles by the American ethicist Richard Deats swelled their ranks. Even so, they were hardly ready for the surprise of 3 November 1985.

Marcos' Announcement and AKKAPKA's Initiatives

On that day, Marcos suddenly announced presidential elections for 7 February 1986. While the ideological left decided to boycott the elections, AKKAPKA quickly devoted all its energy towards trying to guarantee a fair election. They focused on three activities: encouraging the people to vote, preparing poll-watchers, and organising prayer tents.[14]

People intimidated by years of violent governmental

repression needed to be encouraged to cast fear aside, reject government bribes, and vote according to their conscience. Regularly, in previous elections, armed thugs had intimidated voters and stolen ballots. So AKKAPKA joined other religious and civic organisations to help train half a million men and women, young and old, priests and laity, to defend the ballot boxes non-violently even if attacked by armed soldiers or thugs.

AKKAPKA also set up 'prayer tents' in ten highly populated areas. One was located in the heart of Manila's banking community. Day and night, from mid-January 1986 to the end of the crisis, people came to these prayer tents to fast and pray. Hildegard Goss-Mayr, who saw these prayer tents in operation in early 1986, has underlined their importance:

> We cannot emphasize enough the deep spirituality that gave the people the strength to stand against the tanks later on. People prayed every day, for all those who suffered in the process of changing regimes, even for the military, even for Marcos . . . It makes a great difference in a revolutionary process where people are highly emotional whether you promote hatred and revenge or help the people stand firmly for justice without becoming like the oppressor. You want to love your enemy, to liberate rather than destroy him.[15]

Almost immediately after Marcos announced the 'snap' election, more and more people began to call on Cory Aquino, widow of the assassinated Benigno, to challenge Marcos at the polls. Unwilling at first, she reluctantly agreed, announcing her candidacy on 5 December 1985, just two months before the election. In the short, intense campaign, she discovered massive popular support. Clearly she was on her way to a decisive electoral victory.

Marcos, however, used massive, unparalleled fraud to steal the election. According to the Philippine Conference of Catholic Bishops, there was widespread vote-buying, intimidation of voters, dishonest tabulation of the returns, harassment, terrorism and murder.[16] In Metropolitan Manila alone, six hundred thousand people could not vote because Marcos' agents had scrambled the voters' lists.

Tens of thousands of non-violent poll-watchers with NAMFREL courageously placed their bodies in the midst of all this corruption and violence. (In the 1984 parliamentary elections, an independent organisation called NAMFREL had emerged to conduct an independent quick vote count and prevent some of the worst dishonesty.) Strong international support strengthened their hand in the 1986 presidential elections. They deployed their thirty thousand volunteers at the most critical polling stations. Six hundred nuns, nicknamed the 'NAMFREL Marines' went to the most problematic locations. During the day of voting and the subsequent vote count, these non-violent volunteers risked death many times. Twenty-four hours a day, they formed human chains and literally tied themselves to ballot boxes so the boxes could not be stolen.[17]

NAMFREL's quick count showed Cory Aquino with a substantial lead. But the official tabulation placed Marcos ahead. Then, as the parliament (Batasan) prepared to declare Marcos the winner, thirty young computer workers involved in the official vote count left their posts on 9 February to protest the deliberate posting of dishonest returns. That daring act ended any credibility still enjoyed by the official returns.

The Bishops Speak Out

At this desperate moment, the Philippine Catholic Bishops Conference decided to issue one of the more daring political pronouncements of modern times by an official church body. On 13 February, the bishops denounced the elections as fraudulent. They declared that Marcos' government could not command the people's allegiance because it lacked all moral foundation, and they called on the faithful to resist this evil with peaceful non-violence.

'We are not going to effect the change we seek by doing nothing, by sheer apathy,' the bishops insisted. In their pronouncement, read from pulpits all across the country, the bishops dared to propose non-violent resistance:

> Neither do we advocate a bloody, violent means of righting this wrong. If we did, we would be sanctioning the enormous sin of fratricidal strife. Killing to achieve justice is not within the purview of our Christian vision in our present context.
>
> The way indicated to us now is the way of nonviolent struggle for justice.
>
> This means active resistance of evil by peaceful means – in the manner of Christ . . .
>
> We therefore ask every loyal member of the Church, every community of the faithful, to form their judgment about the February 7 polls. And if in faith they see things as we the bishops do, we must come together and discern what appropriate actions to take that will be according to the mind of Christ . . .
>
> These last few days have given us shining examples of the nonviolent struggle for justice we advocate here . . .
>
> Now is the time to speak up. Now is the time to repair the wrong . . . But we insist: Our acting must always be according to the Gospel of Christ, that is, in a peaceful, nonviolent way.[18]

Hildegard Goss-Mayr believes this declaration by the bishops was the first occasion, at least in modern times, when a Catholic Bishops Conference publicly called on the faithful to engage in non-violent civil disobedience to overthrow an unjust system.[19] Cardinal Sin, the Catholic Archbishop of Manila, called it 'the strongest statement any group of bishops has produced anywhere since the days of Henry VIII [in the early sixteenth century]'.[20]

As the bishops' statement reverberated around the Philippines, Cory Aquino was meeting with 350 key advisers to plan a campaign of non-violent resistance. The Goss-Mayrs joined Cory Aquino, Cardinal Sin and others to devise scenarios and develop an extended, non-violent campaign of marches and boycotts designed to overthrow Marcos. A crowd of one million cheering supporters wildly applauded as Mrs Aquino launched her campaign of civil disobedience on 16 February. The tide had turned.[21]

Marcos, however, was determined to stay in power. He announced his intention to meet force with force. The struggle would be long and tough.

'People Power'

But surprise struck again on Saturday evening, 22 February. Unexpectedly Juan Ponce Enrile (Marcos' Minister of Defence) and General Fidel Ramos rebelled. Denouncing the fraudulent elections in a news conference, they declared Mrs Aquino the rightful President, and at 9.00 p.m., with only two hundred armed defenders, they barricaded themselves inside their camps in the middle of Metropolitan Manila. Their two hundred soldiers were at the mercy of Marcos' army of 250,000. The President could destroy them at will.

At that moment, Butz Aquino and Cardinal Sin unleashed 'people power'. Late on Saturday night, Butz Aquino called cause-orientated groups to fill the streets outside Enrile's and Ramos' campus. 'We will surround the camps and protect them with our bodies,' he announced boldly.[22]

Cardinal Sin went on the radio Saturday evening and urged the people to surround the camps. 'Go to Camp Aguinaldo and show your solidarity' with Ramos and Enrile, 'our two good friends', the Cardinal pleaded.[23] Within hours, thousands of men, women and children ringed the gates of the camps, blocking any potential movement by Marcos' army. Marcos would have to kill civilians if he chose to attack.

Before he went on the radio, Cardinal Sin called three orders of nuns. To each, he said: 'Right now get out from your cells and go to the chapel and pray . . . And fast until I tell you to stop. We are in battle.'[24] No troops attacked the rebels on Saturday night.

By Sunday morning the streets around the camps were overflowing with people. Families came with children and picnic baskets. In spite of the danger, the mood was festive. All over the city, taxi and truck drivers spontaneously volunteered to shuttle people to the scene of action. Ramos and Enrile went on the air to beg for more civilians to flood the streets to act as a buffer between themselves and Marcos' soldiers. They fully expected an attack. According to a professor at the Philippine Military Academy, it was this surge of 'people power' that made the difference. 'It was the first time in history', Lieutenant Colonel Purificacion said, 'that so many civilians went to protect the military.'[25]

The non-violent soldiers of this 'classless revolution'

came from every walk of life.[26] Rich bankers, top executives and business men drove their cars to the camps. The poor walked. Men and women, children and grandparents, priest and nuns, flooded the streets. Pregnant women with babies in their arms came ready to defy advancing tanks.

Sunday afternoon at 3.00 p.m. the tanks came. A large force of marines with tanks and armoured personnel carriers headed for Enrile and Ramos' little band of rebels. Rumbling through the streets, the huge machines stopped only a kilometre from Ramos' headquarters, blocked by thousands of bodies ready to die rather than let them continue.

Amado L. Lacuesta, Jr, just one of the hundreds of thousands of civilians in the streets, offers a powerful eyewitness account of the people's raw courage.[27] As he squeezed his way through the densely packed street, he finally got close to where General Tadiar of the marines was negotiating with the civilians who totally surrounded his tanks and armoured personnel carriers (APC). The sea of kneeling people were praying, some holding small statues of the Virgin Mary. General Tadiar demanded that the people let him through, but they refused. Just then Butz Aquino arrived, clambered up on the APC and explained how people power could avoid bloodshed.

As the soldiers pushed Aquino off the huge machine, its engines roared. Weeping and praying, the people expected to be crushed. At the very front were three nuns, kneeling in prayer an arm's length from the throbbing motors. The metal mountain jerked forward once, twice, then stopped. The crowd cheered wildly. As a military helicopter made a low sweep, the people offered cigarettes to the soldiers, who looked away with a mixture of disdain and uncertainty. Again the engines roared and the machine jerked forward. Men pushed against the advancing metal wall as the nuns continued to kneel in prayer. Row after row of densely packed bodies stood ready to be pulverised by tons of metal. But again the towering monster halted. This time, after more hesitation, the APC swivelled and retreated to the deafening roar of thousands of relieved cheering voices.

Cardinal Sin tells the story of bedridden, eighty-one year old Mrs Monzon, owner of Arellano University. Everywhere she went, she used a wheelchair. But Mrs Monzon insisted on joining the people in the streets in front of the camps. When the tanks came, she wheeled in front of the advancing monsters. Armed with a crucifix, she called out to the soldiers: 'Stop. I am an old woman. You can kill me, but you shouldn't kill your fellow Filipinos.' Overcome, a soldier jumped off the tank and embraced the bold non-violent resister. 'I cannot kill you,' he told her, 'you are just like my mother.' She stayed in the street all night in her wheelchair.[28]

The marines finally withdrew without firing a shot.

Monday brought more high drama. At dawn, three thousand marines succeeded in dispersing part of the crowd with tear gas. But seven helicopter gunships with sufficient firepower to obliterate both Ramos' rebel troops and the surrounding crowds landed peacefully and defected. At 9.00 a.m. Marcos appeared defiantly on television for a few minutes and then disappeared as rebel solders seized Channel 4 TV.

Romeo Lavella, Jr, who lived near Channel 4, tells what he saw just after rebels seized the station.[29] Hearing scattered gun shots, he rushed into the streets where swarms of people stood between two groups of heavily armed soldiers. The pro-Marcos loyalists had more than twice as many men as the rebels who had just seized the station.

As sporadic gunfire erupted, a pick-up truck with a priest praying loudly slowly inched forward. As he prayed the Rosary and sang the Ave Maria, the people did the same. In the truck were statues of the crucified Christ and the Virgin Mary. Awed, the soldiers stopped shooting. As another priest and civilians helped negotiate an agreement between the soldiers, the priest and people continued to pray and sing. Channel 4, meanwhile, stayed in the hands of the people.

Hundreds of thousands jammed the streets in front of the camps on Monday. From Cardinal Sin's four auxiliary bishops to unknown slum-dwellers, the people defied the guns and tanks.

One particularly striking encounter occurred in front of the Polymedic Hospital near the camps. Several trucks with gun-wielding soldiers and two APCs slipped past the crowd by displaying yellow streamers (Cory Aquino's campaign colour). A moment later, however, the crowd discovered their mistake and people rushed to seal the street. Middle-aged ladies prayed loudly as helicopters hovered overhead. As the people stood their ground, the massive machines halted. Nobody would retreat. L. P. Flores' eyewitness account of the soldiers' reactions reveals the mystery of 'people power':

> The people pressed their bodies against the armor. Their faces were pleading but they were clothed in nothing but raw courage. In that decisive and tense moment, the soldiers atop the armored carriers pointed their guns of every make at the crowd but their faces betrayed agony. And I knew then, as the crowd, too, must have discerned: the soldiers did not have the heart to pull the trigger on civilians armed only with their convictions. The pact had been sealed. There was tacit agreement: 'We keep this

street corner, you retreat.' And true enough, the armored carriers rolled back and applause echoed.

The face of that soldier struggling in agony for the decision to shoot or not, on the verge of tears, will forever remain in my memory.[30]

Dozens, indeed hundreds, of similar personal struggles ended with soldiers accepting flowers and embracing civilians. The battle was over. By Monday afternoon, a majority of the armed forces had abandoned Marcos. On Tuesday morning, Marcos stubbornly went through an inaugural ceremony, but his power had evaporated. Late that evening, he fled. Mrs Aquino was President.

Evaluating a Non-violent Success

It would be naive, of course, to suppose that unarmed civilians in the streets singlehandedly overthrew Marcos. International pressure (including President Reagan's belated decision to abandon Marcos) and the revolt of the army were clearly important. According to an editorial in the *Philippine Daily Inquirer*, however, it was massive non-violent resistance that made the difference.

When the revolution now popularly called People Power began, it was triggered by two Filipinos – Juan Ponce Enrile and Fidel Ramos. But neither of them would have survived if the people had not put themselves between the attackers and the leaders of the revolt.

People all over the world then saw the unbelievable.

Filipinos charging at giant tanks with Volkswagens. Nuns and priests meeting armored cars with Rosaries and prayers. Little children giving grim soldiers flowers and urging them not to fight for Marcos. People linking arms and blocking tanks, daring them to crush their fellow Filipinos, which they did not.[31]

Reading through the many eyewitness accounts in
*An Eyewitness History: People Power, The Philippine
Revolution of 1986*, one is amazed by the centrality of
prayer and religious devotion. Sister Teresa was one of
the Carmelite nuns ordered to fast and pray by Cardinal
Sin. 'We never forgot even for an instant that we were
doing battle. We daily called God in prayer to assist us
all: those outside and we inside.' The radio accounts of
the struggle in the streets, Sr Teresa confessed, shaped
their prayers.[32]

Praying nuns and non-violent resisters armed only
with religious symbols had obviously functioned as an
effective deterrent:

> People were willing to die but not to kill. And I thought
> that even if some soldiers were willing to shoot the people,
> they were not willing to shoot the crucifixes. Many of them
> come from the provinces where they were raised to fear
> God. They could never shoot at people who were praying.
> They could have shot people who were throwing stones, as
> they did during the rallies. But this was the first time that
> they were confronted with prayers. They did not know how
> to react. I think this was crucial to the whole nonviolence
> stance.
>   The people were there to defend the camp. They were not
> aggressors. We cannot pray and be violent at the same
> time. The religious character of the revolution made the
> revolution very unique. If you took away the religious
> flavor of the revolution, you would have removed the
> essence of it.[33]

Professor Randolf David, Director of Third World
Studies at the University of the Philippines, concluded
in amazement: 'I have been a student of revolutions, but
this is the first time I have seen an assault led by the
Virgin Mary.'[34]

Undoubtedly the previous training in non-violence
had played a genuine role, although the convergence of

the masses to protect the rebel soldiers was essentially a spontaneous emotional response rather than the result of careful organising. Not surprisingly, non-violent leaders like Father Jose Blanco, the founder of AKKAPKA, believe the Philippine revolution points the way for the rest of the world:

> What does God wish us to proclaim to the world through our nonviolent revolution? Simply this: the political problems of people can be solved without recourse to arms or violence.
> The world's problems are best solved if we respect the humanity, the dignity of every human person concerned. The desire to be violent or to use violence can be tamed and diminished, if we show love, care, joy to those who are unjust and wish to be violent. Violence addresses the aggressor. Nonviolence searches out and addresses the humanity in the enemy or oppressor. When that common humanity is touched, then the other is helped to recognize the human person within and ceases to be inhuman, unjust, and violent.
> One does not have to be a Christian to reach out to the humanity in the other.[35]

Such optimism needs tempering. One successful non-violent revolution does not banish war. Nor dare one overlook the special circumstances that helped non-violence succeed in this unique situation. Furthermore, simply overthrowing Marcos did not create economic justice in the Philippines. A year and a half later, it is still unclear whether President Cory Aquino will be able to correct the structural injustice that has created so much poverty in her country.

But the Filipino people did depose a powerful dictator with virtually no bloodshed. Precisely in a context where many had concluded that the only viable path was years of bloody revolution, non-violence produced a stunning victory. Non-violent revolution *is* possible.

PART II:

A CALL TO ACTION

4   MULTIPLYING SUCCESS

Most movements of social change have only begun to
experiment with the real power and flexibility of
nonviolence . . . One of the greatest discoveries of this
century is in the real power of mass nonviolent
movements.

Richard B. Deats[1]

Now is the time to test the limits and possibilities of
non-violent resistance to injustice and oppression. The
Christian community has never done that in a sustained, carefully organised and solidly financed way.
Nor has any other community. In the late twentieth
century, however, there are compelling reasons for
experimenting with non-violence on a scale never before attempted in human history.

Why We Must Seriously Explore Non-violent Alternatives

The sheer success of numerous non-violent campaigns
in itself warrants increased exploration and implementation. The previous chapters have chronicled story
after story where even spontaneous, ill-prepared non-
violent resistance succeeded beyond anyone's wildest
dreams.

Furthermore, non-violent campaigns have again and
again proved more effective than lethal violence. That

is true in the very specific sense that they have accomplished their goals with far less loss of life than their violent alternatives.

When one compares the numbers of people who died in the campaigns for independence in India and Algeria, the figures are astonishing. India's non-violent struggle for independence from the British took longer than Algeria's violent victory over French colonialism (twenty-eight years, from 1919–1946, compared to seven years, from 1955–1961). But only eight thousand Indians died, whereas a million Algerian lives were lost. Even more staggering is the comparison of the numbers of dead with total population figures. Of India's three hundred million, only 1 in 400,000 died. Of Algeria's ten million, 1 in 10 was sacrificed.[2]

Solidarity in Poland accomplished more in combatting Marxist totalitarianism than did Argentina in the Falklands/Malvinas War against democratic England. But only three hundred Poles died, whereas Argentina lost a thousand in two weeks. Less than a hundred died (fifty thousand more were jailed) in the American civil rights movement. In the Cuban revolution, twenty thousand died. There were at least that many deaths (and probably more) in the Nicaraguan revolution against Somosa.[3]

One understands why Senator Benigno Aquino of the Philippines turned away from violence after a comparative study of violent and non-violent revolutions. The twentieth century has demonstrated that non-violent revolutions can be more effective.

The past century of carnage and the future prospects of much worse to come also compel us to search for non-violent alternatives. The twentieth century has been the most bloody in human history. A nuclear holocaust would make all past bloodshed seem like child's play. The ever-upward spiral of violence and counter-violence seems not only unending but ever more colossal in its destructive dimensions. Surely at a time like this, an exploration of non-violent alternatives must be high on everyone's agenda.

In May 1983, I was one of the speakers at a large conference in California on 'The Church and Peacemaking in the Nuclear Age'. In my speech, I proposed the kind of non-violent peace team on the Honduras–Nicaragua border that took shape later that year with Witness for Peace.[4] What surprised me was the positive response of another speaker, General Robert Mathis, who had recently retired as Chief of the US Air Force. Subsequent conversation helped me understand why General Mathis liked my proposal. General Mathis is so terrified by what he knows about the deadly dangers posed by nuclear weapons that he is eager to explore any realistic approach that offers non-violent alternatives for resolving international conflict. That is not to claim that large numbers of top military leaders will quickly join a coalition to implement non-violence. Such a claim would be naive. But the episode does indicate that the desire for non-violent alternatives is more widespread and urgent in our time.

Still another reason for serious testing of non-violence is that it is more democratic and therefore less subject to abuse. A non-violent struggle involves large numbers rather than a handful of highly trained, well-equipped élites who consequently possess enormous power after their violent revolution has succeeded. Gandhi pointed out that 'in nonviolence the masses have a weapon which enables a child, a woman, or even a decrepit old man to resist the mightiest government successfully'.[5]

The Nobel Peace Prize winner Adolfo Perez Esquivel

underlines this strength of non-violence with his humorous discussion of the 'battle of the elephant and the ants'. 'True the elephant is stronger. But the ants ... well, there are more of us.'[6] Hence the repeated success of non-violent masses, even when pitted against powerful and ruthless military machines.

But the virtue of non-violence lies not only in the fact that it enables unarmed masses to conquer armed opponents. It is also that there is a better chance of democratic results after the revolution, precisely because the process itself is more democratic. When small, armed élites have seized power, even in the name of 'justice for the people', the result has very often been further repression. One need only think of Stalin in Russia, Mao in China, Ben Bella in Algeria, Castro in Cuba, and Pinochet in Chile. Once chosen, violence is not easily abandoned. Violent revolution by an armed élite is one of the least effective training grounds for democratic cooperation.

Advocates of non-violence have sometimes been accused of naivete about human nature and the pervasive power of evil. But David Hoekema turns this argument on its head, precisely at the point of the abuse of lethal weapons intended only to restrain evil.

> The reality of human sinfulness means that the instruments we intend to use for good are certain to be turned to evil purposes as well. There is therefore a strong presumption for using those means of justice that are least likely to be abused and least likely to cause irrevocable harm when they are abused.[7]

A popular non-violent revolution increases the prospects of a democratic future. Its very nature prevents the emergence of small armed élites who consequently possess enormous power that is regularly abused. At the same time, non-violence schools large numbers of people in the tough skills of political struggle and respect for the humanity even of opponents.[8] The tragedy of Karl Marx is not that he saw the reality of class conflict, but rather that his way of solving the problem elevated conflict to a necessary law of history.[9] Rather than exacerbating conflict between groups in a society, on the contrary, non-violence reduces the hostility. That in turn makes more possible a future society where all can coexist in relative harmony, freedom and justice.

In the light of these compelling reasons for a new, sustained exploration of the possibilities of non-violence, it is not surprising that more and more official church documents have recently issued the call. Even so, the number and diversity are impressive.

Church Leaders' Calls For Non-violent Options

The Latin American Catholic bishops appealed for non-violence in their official statements at Puebla in 1979: 'Our responsibility as Christians is to use all possible means to promote the implementation of nonviolent tactics in the effort to re-establish justice in economic and political relations.'[10] One commentator concluded that at Puebla, conservative, moderate and progressive thinkers agreed that 'the future struggle in Latin America will depend on ... the techniques used by Martin Luther King and Mahatma Gandhi'.[11]

In 1983, Belgian and Dutch Catholic bishops both affirmed the importance of non-violence. In July, the Belgian bishops said: 'Maybe the Church of earlier times and of today should have given more emphasis to the witness of nonviolence.'[12] In May, the Dutch bishops had been more emphatic: 'The development of methods which enable people to resist injustice and to defend themselves without using violence is in keeping with the spirit of the Gospel and may not be labelled as utopian and unrealistic.'[13]

In their widely acclaimed peace pastoral of the same year, the US Catholic bishops spoke even more vigorously. Noting that Vatican II had praised those who renounce the use of violence in favour of other methods of defence, they insisted: 'Non-violent means of resistance to evil deserve much more study and consideration than they have thus far received. There have been significant instances in which people have successfully resisted oppression without recourse to arms. Non-violence is not the way of the weak, the cowardly, or the impatient.'[14]

At the conclusion of this lengthy appeal for developing non-violent means of conflict resolution, the bishops declared: 'No greater challenge or higher priority can be imagined than the development and perfection of a theology of peace suited to a civilization poised on the brink of self-destruction.'[15]

Three years later, the United Methodist bishops added their voice to the list of official church appeals for a more vigorous exploration of non-violence. Citing Harvard University's Gene Sharp and Witness for Peace, they said: 'We encourage special study of non-violent defense and peacemaking forces.'[16]

Unlike the Catholic and Methodist bishops, the National Association of Evangelicals has been largely supportive of current nuclear policy. Their *Guidelines: Peace, Freedom and Security Studies*, issued in1986, unhesitatingly offers an ethical defence of nuclear weapons. But even in this document, one finds a repeated call for 'alternatives to violence in world politics'.[17] In a section on 'Change without Violence', they pledge to 'study and seek ways to apply that spectrum of possibilities for change without violence that runs from nonviolent forms of social organization for the defense of values to new concepts of communication and conflict resolution'.[18]

In December 1986 the Mennonite and Brethren in Christ Churches of North America completed an extensive two-year exploration of a proposal to establish peacemaking teams trained to intervene in situations of violent conflict using the techniques of King and Gandhi. Abandoning the category of 'nonresistance' as the dominant definition of their pacifism, they called for 'caring, direct challenge of evil'. And they endorsed the establishment, training and deployment of Christian Peacemaker Teams using non-violent direct action.[19]

Common Ground for Pacifists and Non-Pacifists

Non-violence is clearly on the Christian church's agenda in a dramatic new way. Not only historic Anabaptist pacifists but also Catholics and Protestants in the just war tradition are calling for a new exploration of non-violence. In fact, as the US Catholic bishops point out, non-violent resistance offers 'a common ground of agreement' between Christians who stand in the just war tradition and those who stand in the pacifist tradition.[20]

In fact, one must put it much more strongly. To have any integrity, both the pacifist and just war traditions demand a massive commitment to non-violence.

According to the just war tradition, lethal violence must always be a last resort. How then can Christians

in the just war tradition claim that they are justified in
resorting to war until they have devoted vast amounts
of time and money to explore the possibilities of non-
violence? In a century where Martin Luther King and
Mahatma Gandhi are two of the most revered international religious leaders; in a century where success
after success has been registered in non-violent campaigns against oppression, injustice and dictatorship; at
such a time, no one can honestly deny that non-violence
is often a realistic alternative to war or violent revolution. The only way that the just war criterion of 'last
resort' can have any integrity at all in our time is if
Christians in that tradition commit themselves to a
sophisticated and sustained testing of the possibilities
of non-violent alternatives.[21]

Pacifist premises demand a similar commitment.
Pacifists hotly reject the charge that their refusal to
bear arms is a callous or cowardly disregard of their
obligation to defend the weak and defenceless against
bullies and tyrants. If pacifists think they have an
alternative to war, then they must have the guts and
integrity to prove it in the brutal world of Hitlers,
Somosas, Pinochets and Pol Pots. If pacifists are not
ready to run the same risk as soldiers in non-violent
struggle against evil, they have no moral right to pretend that they know a better way. Only pacifists ready
to risk death by the thousands will have credibility in a
century that has witnessed the greatest bloodshed in
human history. Costly pacifist involvement in successful non-violent campaigns is perhaps the most effective
way to convince doubting contemporaries that there is
an alternative to war. Pacifist premises and goals demand a much more vigorous commitment to non-
violent defence of freedom, justice and peace.

A new non-violent movement in the Christian church

possesses a twofold virtue. It offers the promise of greater integrity to the stated positions of both pacifist and just war Christians. It also offers a channel, not for ending their ongoing debate, but for throwing the emphasis on mutual cooperation in non-violent resistance as both focus on what the US Catholic bishops have rightly called the 'common ground of agreement'.[22]

A Call For a New Exploration of Non-violent Alternatives

Now is the time to move from spontaneous, ill-prepared non-violent skirmishes to a serious and sustained global exploration of the full power of non-violent alternatives. Harvard's Gene Sharp, probably the most important contemporary analyst of non-violence, underlines the difference:

Nonviolent action has almost always been improvised without significant awareness of the past history of this type of struggle. It has usually been waged without qualified leadership, or without . . . wide popular understanding of the technique, without thorough comprehension of its requirements for effectiveness, without preparations and training, without analyses of past conflicts, without studies of strategy and tactics, without a consciousness among the actionists that they were waging a special type of struggle. In short, the most unfavorable circumstances possible have accompanied the use of this technique. It is amazing that the significant number of victories for nonviolent struggle exist at all, for these conditions of the lack of knowledge, skill and preparations have been to the highest degree unfavorable.

In contrast, for many centuries military struggle has benefited from conscious efforts to improve its effectiveness in all the ways in which nonviolent action has lacked.[23]

Many today honestly believe we must maintain massive nuclear and non-nuclear weaponry. Others disagree. Without settling that disagreement, however, both can unite in a new exploration of the possibilities and limits of non-violence. Could we not all agree that it would be worthwhile to see what would happen if for two decades we spent at least one-tenth as much on non-violent methods as we do on preparation for lethal violence? Concretely that would mean massive new activity in at least three areas: study centres to analyse the history of previous non-violent successes and failures; training centres to prepare large numbers of people in the strategy and tactics of actual non-violent campaigns; and the launching of new non-violent movements. In different ways, study centres, training centres and actual campaigns would all serve to popularise the possibilities of non-violence.

Study centres

Harvard University's Program on Nonviolent Sanctions in Conflict and Defense offers a model that ought to be duplicated at scores of colleges and universities around the world. Directed by Dr Gene Sharp and located in Harvard's Center for International Affairs, the Program on Nonviolent Sanctions attracts a growing circle of scholars. They are producing an expanding stream of articles and books that offer detailed analyses of specific non-violent campaigns, comparative studies of tactics, methods and outcomes, and theoretical analyses of power and politics from the perspective of non-violence.[24]

If the Christian church is serious about exploring non-violence, then we must develop financial resources and the scholars to make possible scores of new study centres on non-violence around the world. Individuals, foundations and denominations can provide the money. Colleges and universities can develop the centres to produce both scholarly studies and popular materials.[25]

Training centres

We also need new training centres. We saw in chapter 3 how important were the short-term training institutes conducted for key Philippine leadership by the Goss-Mayrs. The Fellowship of Reconciliation sponsors training seminars and Witness for Peace does short training sessions for its volunteers. Other modest training programmes exist and limited materials have been prepared.[26] But much more is required. We need a number of action-orientated training centres that can produce trained non-violent activists familiar with the tactics of Gandhi and King, and ready to lead non violent campaigns.

Some training centres could concentrate on producing generalists – trainers of trainers. Others could prepare people for specific campaigns like Witness for Peace and/or new ventures. In both cases, key components would include spiritual formation and the techniques of non-violent direct action. The development of a biblical spirituality of prayer, Bible study and worship focused on the heavy emotional demands of costly non-violent intervention would be essential. Each volunteer should be supported by a 'home-town' support group and prayer chain committed to regular prayer plus all-night intercession during emergencies.

All the concrete strategies, techniques and tactics learnt in the many campaigns of King, Gandhi and others need to be studied carefully.[27] Role-playing scenarios of intervention, ambush, crowd control and injury would be important. When training for action in a specific locale, extensive study of the geography, history, economics, politics and culture of the area would be an additional crucial component.

New non-violent movements

Launching new non-violent movements is so difficult as to seem almost impossible. But congregations, denominations and interdenominational bodies could decide to call, train and equip new teams familiar with the history, theory and tactics of non-violence and ready to move into situations of violent conflict. Such teams could reduce both killing and oppression by their direct intervention and also serve as the trainers and catalysts for provoking the widespread adoption of non-violent methods by much larger numbers of people. In the last chapter, we saw that the Mennonites of North America had decided to launch new Christian Peacemaker Teams ready to intervene peacefully in conflict situations both in North America and abroad. If violence is truly to be a last resort for churches in the just war tradition, then they will need to do the same.

Could not the Christian church set the target of training, by the year 1995, five thousand volunteers per year for an ever-expanding, worldwide Christian peace brigade? Trained volunteers could spend one to three years in new non-violent campaigns all around the world. A growing body of 'non-violent reserves' would be available for special emergencies.

Frequently, these teams would work in their own country and culture. Frequently, too, however, as Peace Brigades International and Witness for Peace have shown, international teams would be desirable and effective.

Non-violent Strategies, Tactics and Principles

It is impossible in a book such as this to describe the precise scenarios for the actual intervention of Christian Peacemaker Teams. But we do know the places where they are needed as well as the places where new groupings and proposals for non-violent intervention are emerging. An extremely creative new non-violent proposal for the struggle against apartheid has just appeared.[28] Non-violent tactics are increasingly being explored by Palestinians on the West Bank in Israel.[29] As this book goes to press, a substantially non-violent campaign in the West Bank has captured world headlines for several months. In South Africa, black Church leaders are making plans for a new Church-based non-violent campaign against apartheid. A hundred other places of violent agony from Sri Lanka to Northern Ireland to El Salvador cry out for non-violent alternatives.

While the specific tactics of Christian Peacemaker Teams (CPTs) in all these places cannot be decided abstractly ahead of time, certain general principles and criteria of intervention are fairly clear.

- CPTs would be *non-partisan in outlook* and not seek to promote or destroy any nation or group, although in specific situations a particular aspect of the policy of one nation or group would be challenged.
- Therefore CPTs would always, at every phase of their activity, *seek to establish and maintain dialogue* with all parties to a conflict. They would never attempt to impose a specific political, constitutional or economic proposal, but rather seek to create a context where the warring parties themselves could peacefully negotiate solutions appropriate for their unique setting.

- At the same time, CPTs would not be indifferent to the biblical call for justice and freedom for all people. Therefore, CPTs would always *seek to act in ways that promote religious and political freedom*, including freedom of worship, speech, democratic elections and equality before the law. They would also *seek to foster economic justice* where all are genuinely free to enjoy adequate food, housing, clothing, education, health care and meaningful work to earn their own keep.

  Several criteria for intervention would be basic.
- CPTs would intervene only after a careful attempt to dialogue with, understand and affirm the legitimate concerns of all parties to a conflict.
- CPTs would intervene only after at least one major party in the conflict had issued an invitation and agreed to give them the freedom to operate in their area.
- CPTs would always seek to operate in the territory of both sides to a conflict, and would decide to operate exclusively in the territory of one side only after their offer to operate on both sides had been rejected.
- CPTs would intervene only when they believed that they could operate non-violently in a way that would probably promote peace, justice and freedom.
- CPTs would place a high priority on sharing the vision and techniques of non-violence with the people wherever they serve.

What kinds of interventions might be possible for CPTs? The history of non-violent action suggests a wide variety of possibilities.

Interpositioning involves placing oneself between two warring parties. Perhaps the most dramatic interpositioning has occurred in India where Gandhi and then the Shanti Sena movement intervened physically be-

tween rioting Hindu and Muslim mobs. Interpositioning can occur in a number of ways:
- *patrolling* demarcation lines, demilitarised zones or
  borders to deter invasion, violations or disturbances.
- *denying access* to certain areas or buildings (e.g. a
  town under attack by guerrillas, as in the beginnings
  of Witness for Peace in Northern Nicaragua).
- *separating hostile groups* (e.g. Hindus and Moslems
  engaged in inter-religious killing).
- *disarming persons or groups* (a Quaker team did this
  during the struggle of Native Americans at Wounded
  Knee).[30]
- *protecting persons or groups* by living and travelling
  with them (as in the case of Peace Brigades International in Honduras).

Not all non-violent direct action involves physically
placing oneself between two warring parties. It is
totally impossible for fifty or even five hundred volunteers in Witness for Peace in Nicaragua to physically
stand between Nicaragua's almost three million civilians and twelve thousand guerrillas. Much of their
work has been to *record and report* the many instances
of torture, kidnapping and death. Of course, interpositioning is also involved, since careful documentation is possible only if one is present in the battle zone.
However, the primary focus is not on preventing
attacks by interposing one's body, but rather on chang-
ing public opinion through more accurate information
about the atrocities.

CPTs might also engage in *temporary police work* in a
destabilised situation. This might happen if CPTs replaced an *ad hoc* military force or even a United Nations
military unit. (This seemed possible in Cyprus in
1973.)[31]

Perhaps some new non-violent tactic might be found

to intervene to *dramatise* the evil of apartheid. What would happen if Billy Graham, the Archbishop of Canterbury and Pope John Paul II led an international team of CPTs to join a new inter-racial campaign of non-violence within South Africa?

Interpositioning, documentation and reporting, temporary police work and dramatisation of injustice would all be possible types of intervention for CPTs.

But would they ever succeed? What is the basis of power of non-violent action?[32]

The Power of Non-violence

Too often, power is understood only in terms of lethal coercion. (Mao said power is what comes from the barrel of a gun.) Certainly power includes the ability to control people's actions by the threat or use of lethal violence. But the people also possess non-violent collective power because they can choose to withdraw their support from rulers. The political scientist Karl Deutsch points out that 'the voluntary or habitual compliance of the mass of the population is the invisible but very real basis of the power of every government'.[33] The potential choice by large numbers to withdraw that compliance represents enormous collective power. Consequently, without any arms at all, the people can exercise non-violent power either by doing what they are not expected or required to do or by refusing to do what they are expected to do.[34] Large numbers of people using non-violent techniques possess enormous non-violent collective power.

But non-violence does not require large numbers to have power. Witness for Peace and Peace Brigades International have demonstrated that even small groups can exercise substantial power.

Non-violent activists possess strong moral power. Praying, reconciling CPTs risking their lives for others would share something of the moral power Jesus exercised in the temple. He was able single-handedly to drive the crowds of angry, oppressive moneychangers out of the temple, not because he was stronger or his disciples were more numerous: it was because deep in their hearts they knew he was right.

International public opinion would also be powerful. The daring of the CPTs would sometimes be headline news around the world. Any group or nation that battered or killed prominent, internationally famous Christian leaders or even ordinary members of CPTs would suffer substantial international disapproval.

A mandate also provides authority and therefore power. A mandate to intervene internationally, if issued by an organisation such as the Organization of African States or the United Nations, could legitimise CPTs. So too – at least to a certain, if lesser, degree – would an invitation by prominent Christian leaders and established churches, as well as recognised leaders of other religious groups.

Self-sacrificial love weakens even vicious opponents. Though not always of course. People ready to suffer for others sometimes get crucified. But often, too, they evoke a more human, loving response, even from brutal foes.

The discipline, training and coordination of an organised body with visible symbols of identity and cohesion are also powerful. Part of the power of a large group of police or soldiers lies in their uniforms, careful coordination and ability to act quickly, decisively and collectively. Highly trained and disciplined CPTs would possess some of this same power.

Finally, there is the divine power of the Lord of

history. What the Almighty will do if thousands of praying, loving Christians non-violently face death in the search for peace and justice will remain shrouded in mystery – at least until we have the courage to try it. But what believer will doubt that there may be surprises ahead?

We do have to be honest and realistic. We never dare pretend that no one would get hurt. Tyrants and bullies callously torture and murder. Opponents would intimidate, threaten, wound, torture and massacre even praying CPTs. But we have always assumed that death by the thousands, indeed even millions, is necessary in war. Would it not be right for non-violent CPTs to be ready to risk death in the same way soldiers do? Certainly we must not seek death. Martyr complexes are wrong. But a readiness to lay down one's life for others lies at the heart of the gospel.

Death will be tragically intertwined with any serious test of the effectiveness of non-violence. But that will not prove that the effort has failed. It will only underline the depth of human sin. And also the fact that Christians are willing to imitate the One they worship.

5   THE MORAL EQUIVALENT OF WAR

> The War against war is going to be no holiday excursion or camping party.
>
> William James[1]

In a now famous essay, 'The Moral Equivalent of War', William James argued that the struggle for non-violent alternatives would be a long and costly battle. Why? Because 'history is a bath of blood'.[2] War has been central to human history because violent instincts are deeply embedded in the human heart.

The costly demands of non-violent action

Anyone seeking to reduce war, James argued, must realise that in important respects war represents human nature at its best. Not only does war smash the dull boredom of ordinary life, it also summons forth high virtues such as courage, self-sacrifice, intense discipline and total dedication. War disciplines the slack, rewards the daring, evokes one's last ounce of energy and breeds loyalty to the larger community. How, James concluded, can any peace movement succeed unless it offers meaningful substitutes for the glamour and appeal of war?

If James' essay poses a valid question, then vigorous non-violent action offers the answer. Non-violent re-

sistance to tyrants, oppressors and brutal invaders is
not for fools or cowards. It demands courage and daring
of the highest order. It requires discipline, training and
a willingness to face death. It produces collective pride
in the group or society that successfully, as in the
Philippines, stands together and overcomes a brutal
foe.

Are there tough, brave volunteers for that kind of
costly, demanding battle? Would the people be there if
the Christian church – and people of other faiths as well
– called for a vast multiplication of our efforts in non-
violent alternatives to war? Would the scholars and
trainees emerge if we doubled and then quadrupled our
study and training centres on non-violence? Would the
non-violent troops be available to be trained by the
thousands and then tens of thousands to form disciplined Christian Peacemaker Teams ready to walk into
the face of danger and death in loving confrontation of
injustice and oppression? We will not know until
courageous Christian leaders, organisations and denominations decide to issue the call and spend the
money.

But the time has never been more right. At no time in
history, perhaps, has the concrete evidence of the tang-
ible success of non-violence been clearer. At no time has
the need to break the escalating cycle of violence and
counter-violence been greater. As late twentieth-
century people glance back in anguish at history's most
violent century and peer ahead fearfully to far worse
potential catastrophes, a new sustained exploration
of the possibilities of non-violence seems to be a
prerequisite of sanity.

The ultimate risk

But the battle will be long and costly. To argue that
non-violence is less costly in human lives than is warfare is not to pretend that no one will be wounded or
killed. Some will die. Everyone must be ready to face
death.

Are there enough people for such a struggle? The
history of warfare and of non-violent action proves that
danger does not deter volunteers. Throughout history,
millions of bold souls have gladly risked death for a
noble cause and a grand vision. Walter Wink is surely
right that 'there is a whole host of people simply waiting
for the Christian message to challenge them for once to
a heroism worthy of their lives'.[3]

Death of course, is not the point. To seek martyrdom
would be naive and immoral. The way of Christ is the
way of life, not death. But the Christian martyrs of all
ages provide testimony that the way to abundant life
sometimes passes through the dark valley where the
cross stands stark and rugged. Those who dare in loving
obedience to shoulder that old rugged cross will ex-
change it some day for a crown of *shalom* in the peaceful
kingdom of the reconciling Lamb.

NOTES

Introduction

1 Quoted in Adolfo Perez Esquivel, *Christ in a Poncho: Testimonials of the Nonviolent Struggles of Latin America*, ed. Charles Antoine, trans. Robert R. Barr (Maryknoll, NY: Orbis Books, 1983), p. 87.
2 Gene Sharp, *The Politics of Nonviolent Action*, 3 vols (Boston: Porter Sargent Publishers, 1973), 1., p. 98.
3 See the helpful discussion and literature cited in Duane K. Friesen, *Christian Peacemaking and International Conflict: A Realist Pacifist Perspective* (Scottdale, PA: Herald Press, 1986), pp. 143–157.
4 Sharp, *Politics of Nonviolent Action*, 2., pp. 117–435.
5 I have dealt with national self-defence in Part 4 of Ronald J. Sider and Richard K. Taylor, *Nuclear Holocaust and Christian Hope* (London: Hodder and Stoughton, 1983), pp. 229–292. Taylor is also working on a book that includes a discussion of non-violent methods for police work.
6 Pastoral Statement of the National Conference of Catholic Bishops, *The Challenge of Peace: God's Promise and Our Response* (Boston: St Paul Editions, 1983), No. 222, p. 58.

Chapter 1: What Exists is Possible

1 Kenneth Boulding, quoted in Jerome D. Frank, *Sanity and Survival: Psychological Aspects of War and Peace* (New York: Vintage Books, 1968), p. 270.
2 Gene Sharp has divided non-violent action into the three broad categories mentioned here: protest and persuasion, non-co-operation, and intervention; see Gene Sharp, *The Politics of Nonviolent Action*, 3 vols (Boston: Porter Sargent Publishers, 1973), 2., pp. 114–448.
   In this book, I focus largely on the third, but all three are dealt with and are in fact inseparably interrelated.
3 Gene Sharp's book (see note 2) is one of the best. See also the Bibliography, especially the books by William Robert Miller

(see note 11) and Anders Boserup and Andrew Mack (see note 37).

4 Josephus, *Wars*, ii. 9., in Hugh R. Trevor-Roper, *Josephus: The Jewish War and Other Selections* (Union Square, NY: Twayne Publishers, Inc., 1965), pp. 201, 202.

5 This story is told by Josephus; see *Antiquities*, xviii. 8. and *Wars*, ii. 10., in Trevor-Roper, *Josephus*.

6 Edward Gibbon, *The Decline and Fall of the Roman Empire*, vol. 2 (New York: Random House, 1954), p. 289.

7 Lanza del Vasto, *Warriors of Peace: Writings on the Technique of Nonviolence* (New York: Alfred A. Knopf, 1974), p. 197.

8 Gibbon, *Decline and Fall*, p. 293. See also, T. Walter Wallbank and Alastair Taylor, *Civilization Past and Present*, vol. 1 (Dallas, TX: Scott, Foresman, 1976), p. 215.

9 Attila was discovered dead in his bed soon after this incident. He had expired during one of his many honeymoon celebrations.

10 Walter H. Conser, Ronald M. McCarthy, David J. Toscano and Gene Sharp (eds), *Resistance, Politics and the American Struggle for Independence, 1765–1775* (Boulder, CO: Lynne Rienner Publishers, 1986).

11 Quoted in William Robert Miller, *Nonviolence: A Christian Interpretation* (New York: Association Press, 1964), p. 239.

12 For the story, see Miller, *Nonviolence*, pp. 230–243 and the short summary in Ronald J. Sider and Richard K. Taylor, *Nuclear Holocaust and Christian Hope* (Downers Grove, IL and Ramsey, NJ: InterVarsity Press/Paulist Press, 1982), pp. 235–237.

13 del Vasto, *Warriors of Peace*, p. 202.

14 Sharp, *Politics of Nonviolent Action*, 1., p. 98.

15 See Charles C. Walker, *A World Peace Guard* (Hyderabad, India: Academy of Gandhian Studies, 1981), p. 65, and Allan A. Hunter, *Courage in Both Hands* (New York: Ballantine Books, 1962), p. 90.

16 Walker, *Guard*, p. 65.

17 Quoted in Hunter, *Courage*, p. 92.

18 See the analysis of Weinberg, *Instead of Violence*, p. 303.

19 William James, 'The Moral Equivalent of War', in John K. Roth (ed.), *The Moral Equivalent of War and Other Essays* (New York: Harper & Row, 1971), p. 10.

20 Walker, *Guard*, pp. 65, 66.

21 *Ibid.*, p. 69.

22 Joan Bondurant provides this definition of satyagraha in her classic work *Conquest of Violence: The Gandhian Philosophy of Conflict*, (1958; revised edition, Berkeley, CA: University of

California Press, 1971), p. 16. In his autobiography (trans. Mahadev Desai), Gandhi offers the following interpretation: 'Sat = truth, Agraha = firmness'; see *Gandhi: An Autobiography by Mohandas K. Gandhi* (Boston, MA: Beacon Press, 1957), p. 319.

23   Quoted in Bondurant, *Conquest of Violence*, p. 96.
24   This section is based on Eknath Easwaran, *A Man to Match His Mountains: Badshah Khan, Nonviolent Soldier of Islam* (Petaluma, CA: Nilgiri Press, 1984).
25   *Ibid.*, p. 99.
26   *Ibid.*, p. 20.
27   *Ibid.*
28   *Ibid.*, p. 110.
29   *Ibid.*, p. 111.
30   *Ibid.*, p. 118.
31   *Ibid.*, p. 123.
32   *Ibid.*, p. 126–128.
33   *Ibid.*, p. 175.
34   *Ibid.*, p. 189.
35   *Ibid.*, p. 195.
36   Quoted in George Estey and Doris Hunter, *Nonviolence* (Waltham: Xerox College Publishing, 1971), p. 92.
37   Quoted in Anders Boserup and Andrew Mack, *War Without Weapons: Non-Violence in National Defense* (New York: Schocken Books, 1975), pp. 123–124.
38   Sharp, *Politics of Nonviolent Action*, 1., pp. 79–81.
39   Quoted in Gene Keyes, 'Peacekeeping by Unarmed Buffer Forces: Precedents and Proposals', in *Peace and Change: A Journal of Peace Research* 5/2,3 (1978), pp. 3–4.
40   Walker, *Guard*, p. 67.
41   Quoted in Keyes, 'Peacekeeping', p. 4.
42   Quoted *ibid.*
43   A general turned pacifist, Crozier greatly admired Gandhi and saw the 'Peace Army' as an outgrowth of Gandhian principles.
44   Keyes, 'Peacekeeping', p. 4.
45   See Sider and Taylor, *Nuclear Holocaust*, pp. 238–241 for a summary and the bibliographical sources. See also, Paul Wehr, 'Nonviolent Resistance to Nazism: Norway, 1940–45', *Peace and Change: A Journal of Peace Research* 10/3,4 (1984), pp. 77–95; and Paul Wehr, *Conflict Regulation* (Boulder, CO: Westview Press, 1979), pp. 69–100, which has a good study of the Norwegian communications network.
46   Quoted in Eivine Berggrar, 'Experiences of the Norwegian Church in the War', *The Lutheran World Review* 1/1 (1948), p. 51.

47   See Sider and Taylor, *Nuclear Holocaust*, pp. 242–246 for the sources.

48   Quoted in Nora Levin, *The Holocaust: The destruction of European Jewry, 1933–1945* (New York: Schocken Books, 1973), p. 401.

49   Quoted in Frederick B. Charry, *The Bulgarian Jews and the Final Solution 1940–1944* (Pittsburgh: University of Pittsburgh Press, 1972), p. 90.

50   See Patricia Parkman, *Insurrection Without Arms: The General Strike in El Salvador, 1944* (unpublished PhD dissertation, Temple University, 1980), for this story.

51   Quoted *ibid.*, p. 169.

52   See Sharp, *Politics of Nonviolent Action*, 1., pp. 90–93.

53   See Elizabeth Campuzano *et al.*, *Resistance in Latin America* (Philadelphia: American Friends Service Committee, 1970).

54   Sharp, *Politics of Nonviolent Action*, 1., pp. 98–101.

55   Gene Sharp, 'Philippines Taught Us Lessons of Nonviolence', *Los Angeles Times*, 4 April 1986, Section 2, p. 5.

56   Quoted in Madeleine G. Kalb, 'The U.N.'s Embattled Peacekeeper', *The New York Times Magazine*, 19 December 1982, p. 46.

57   Henry Wiseman, 'The United Nations Peacekeeping: An Historical Overview', in Henry Wiseman (ed.), *Peacekeeping: Appraisals and Proposals* (New York: Pergamon Press, 1983), pp. 23–25.

58   Andrew W. Cordier and Wilder Foote, *The Quest for Peace: The Dag Hammarskjöld Memorial Lectures* (New York: Columbia University Press, 1965), p. 113.

59   The observers served under the UNTSO banner – 'United Nations True Supervision Organization' – in Palestine. UNTSO personnel continue on assignment at the time of writing.

60   Kurt Waldheim, *The Challenge of Peace* (New York: Rawson, Wade Publishers, 1980), p. 135.

61   The United Nations Military Observer Group in India and Pakistan (UNMOGIP) continues to serve, though in a reduced capacity.

62   Kalb, 'Peacekeeper', p. 46, and Sydney D. Bailey, *How Wars End: The United Nations and the Termination of Armed Conflict*, vol. 1 (Oxford: Clarendon Press, 1982), pp. 4, 5.

63   Quoted in Charles C. Walker, *Peacekeeping: 1969* (Philadelphia: Friends Peace Committee, 1969), p. 2.

64   Antony Gilpin, 'Non-Violence in the U.N. Peacekeeping Operations', in Ted Dunn (ed.), *Foundations of Peace and Freedom* (Wales: Salesbury Press, 1975), p. 279.

65 Keyes, 'Peacekeeping', p. 3.
66 Kalb, 'Peacekeeper', p. 48.
67 Indar Jit Rikhye, 'Peacekeeping and Peacemaking', in Wiseman, *Peacekeeping*, p. 6.
68 Quoted in Kalb, 'Peacekeeper', p. 48.
69 Waldheim, *Challenge*, pp. 83–84.
70 *Ibid.*, pp. 93–95.
71 It should be noted, however, that the UNEF II mandate expired in 1979, due largely to a Soviet veto threat in the Security Council.
72 Kalb, 'Peacekeeper', p. 48.
73 P. N. Vanzis, *Cyprus: The Unfinished Agony* (London: Abelard-Schuman, 1977), p. 1.
74 Bailey, *How Wars End*, 1., p. 369.
75 Quoted in Miller, *Nonviolence*, p. 120.
76 *Ibid.*, pp. 119–120 and Walker, *Guard*, pp. 71–72.
77 Walker, *Guard*, pp. 71–72.
78 See Narayan Desai, 'Gandhi's Peace Army: The Shanti Sena Today', *Fellowship*, November 1969, pp. 23–25.
79 See Narayan Desai, 'Intervention in Riots in India', in A. Paul Hare and Herbert H. Blumberg (eds), *Liberation Without Violence: A Third Party Approach* (Totowa, NJ: Roman & Littlefield, 1977), p. 83.
80 Miller, *Nonviolence*, p. 123.
81 Cited in Keyes, 'Peacekeeping', p. 8.
82 Cited in Charles C. Walker, 'Nonviolence in Eastern Africa 1962–1964', in Hare and Blumberg, *Liberation*, p. 157.
83 *Ibid.*, pp. 160–167. For a broader discussion of non-violence in Africa, see Charles C. Walker, 'Nonviolence in Africa', in Severyn T. Bruyn and Paula M. Rayman, (eds). *Nonviolent Action and Social Change* (New York: Irvington Publishers, 1979), pp. 186–212. For another attempt at non-violent peacemaking, see A. Paul Hare (ed.), *Cyprus Resettlement Project: An Instance of International Peacemaking* (Beer Sheva: Ben-Gurion University of the Negev, 1984).
84 For this story, see Richard K. Taylor, *Blockade: A Guide to Non-Violent Intervention* (Maryknoll, NY: Orbis Books, 1977).
85 *Ibid.*, p. xiii.
86 From a PBI brochure; for more information on PBI, write to Charles C. Walker, the Coordinator of Peace Brigades International, at the address in note 89.
87 See *Peace Brigades* ('A publication of Peace Brigades International'), 2/1 (1984).
88 The following information about GAM comes from Philip

McManus, 'Refusing to Disappear', *Fellowship*, July–August 1985, pp. 12–14.

89 For further information, write to PBI, 4722 Baltimore Avenue, Philadelphia, PA 19143, or Charles Walker, Box 199, Cheyney, Pa. 193/9.

90 John P. Adams, *At the Heart of the Whirlwind* (New York: Harper & Row, 1976), p. 119.

91 See Hildegard Goss-Mayr, 'Alagamar: Nonviolent Land Struggle', *IFOR Report*, July 1980, pp. 15–16.

92 Penny Lernoux, *Cry of the People* (New York: Penguin Books, 1982), pp. 313–314.

93 See Lyle Tatum, 'Friendly Presence', in Hare and Blumberg, *Liberation*, pp. 92–101.

94 For King's writings, see the extensive collection in James Melvin Washington (ed.), *A Testament of Hope – The Essential Writings of Martin Luther King, Jr* (San Francisco: Harper & Row, 1986). Stephen Oates has written a comprehensive biography, *Let the Trumpet Sound: The Life of Martin Luther King, Jr* (San Francisco: Harper & Row, 1982). See also the important TV documentary called *Eyes on the Prize*, which was released in 1987, and the companion volume ed. Juan Williams, *Eyes on the Prize: America's Civil Rights Years, 1954–1965* (New York: Viking Penguin, Inc., 1987).

Chapter 2: Non-violent Intervention in Guerrilla Warfare

1 Quoted in Witness for Peace Documentation Project, *Kidnapped by the Contras: The Peace Flotilla on the Rio San Juan, Nicaragua, August 1985* (Washington DC: Witness for Peace Documentation Project, 1985), p. 9.

2 For a longer account of that trip, see Ronald J. Sider, 'Why Me Lord?: Reluctant Reflections on the Trip to Nicaragua', *The Other Side*, May 1985, pp. 20–25.

3 As of February 1987. See *Witness for Peace Newsletter*, February–March 1987, p. 4.

4 I want to thank Dr Arnold Snyder for granting me permission to make generous use of an unpublished paper, 'Witness for Peace in Nicaragua', that he wrote in early 1985. From 15 February–15 December 1984, Arnold was the Coordinator of Witness for Peace in Nicaragua. He is now Assistant Professor of History and Peace Studies at Conrad Grebel College, University of Waterloo, Waterloo, Ontario, Canada.

5 Walter LaFeber, *Inevitable Revolutions: The United States in*

Central America (New York: Norton, 1984), p. 11. See also Richard Millett, *Guardians of the Dynasty: A History of the US Created Guardia Nacional de Nicaragua and the Somoza Family* (Maryknoll, NY: Orbis Books, 1977).

6 LaFeber, *Inevitable Revolutions*, p. 18.

7 See my article 'Why Me Lord?'. For a very critical view of the Sandinistas, see Humberto Belli, *Breaking Faith: The Sandinista Revolution and Its Impact on Freedom and Christian Faith in Nicaragua* (Westchester, IL: Crossway Books, 1985). For a positive evaluation, see James and Kathleen McGinnis, *Solidarity with the People of Nicaragua* (Maryknoll, NY: Orbis Books, 1985), pp. 5–25. See also Mario Vargas Llosa's lengthy study, 'Nicaragua', *The New York Times Magazine*, 28 April 1985, p. 37.

8 In conversations with Arnold Snyder (see n. 4).

9 *New York Times*, February 22, 1985.

10 Figures cited in WFP Documentation Project, *Kidnapped by the Contras*, p. 42.

11 Sider, 'Why Me Lord?', p. 22.

12 See Amnesty International, *Nicaragua: The Human Rights Record* (London: Amnesty International, 1986), pp. 32ff., and Americas Watch, *Human Rights in Nicaragua: 1985–6* (Washington: Americas Watch, 4 March 1986), pp. 86ff.

13 Quoted in Snyder, 'Witness for Peace', p. 5.

14 Cited in WFP Documentation Project, *Kidnapped by the Contras*, p. 40.

15 Snyder, 'Witness for Peace', p. 15.

16 The copy I possess has the title: 'Manual del Compatiente Por La Libertad.'

17 See note 25 below.

18 Snyder, 'Witness for Peace', pp. 19–20. In this whole section, I am relying on Snyder's eyewitness account.

19 *Ibid.*, p. 21.

20 For the following story, see WFP Documentation Project, *Kidnapped by the Contras* (see note 10 above).

21 Quoted in *ibid.*, p. 9.

22 Quoted in *ibid.*, p. 6.

23 Quoted in Snyder, 'Witness for Peace', p. 36.

24 Quoted in WFP Documentation Project, *Kidnapped by the Contras*, p. 47.

25 Estimates published by WFP in a 1986 promotional letter.

26 Quoted in Snyder, 'Witness for Peace', p. 38.

27 A complete evaluation of WFP would go way beyond this brief sketch. Among other things, I believe WFP has been too hesitant to criticise Sandinista violations of human rights and

democratic freedoms. WFP has, however, challenged the Sandinista government a number of times. For example, in meetings with Sandinista officials, including President Ortega, representatives of WFP have criticised various aspects of government policy, including mistreatment of Miskito Indians, failure to provide for conscientious objectors in the draft law, incommunicado detention of prisoners, and President Ortega's trip to the Soviet Union.

When President Ortega suspended certain civil liberties in October 1985, the WFP November–December newsletter said, 'We oppose the decision to suspend civil liberties ... We are deeply saddened by developments in Nicaragua restricting human rights.'

In 1985 and 1986 WFP loaned a staff person, Mary Dutcher, to the Washington Office on Latin America. Using WFP resources, she produced two widely publicised reports entitled 'Nicaragua: Violations of the Laws of War by Both Sides'. These reports criticised human rights violations by both the contras and the Nicaraguan government.

In the summer of 1985, when WFP delegates were kidnapped by the contras, a WFP spokesman, Dennis Marker, criticised several specific Sandinista practices during a nationally televised interview on the McNeil-Lehrer Report.

28   For two other recent treatments of WFP, see Joyce Hollyday, 'The Long Road to Jalapa', and Jim Wallis, 'A Venture of Faith', in Jim Wallis (ed.), *The Rise of Christian Conscience* (New York: Harper & Row, 1987), pp. 30–46.

Chapter 3: Wheelchairs vs Tanks

1   Quoted in Douglas J. Elwood, *Philippine Revolution, 1986: Model of Nonviolent Change* (Quezon City, Philippines: New Day Publishers, 1986), p. 19.

2   For much of the following data, see Ricki Ross, 'Land and Hunger: Philippines', Bread for the World Background Paper, No. 55, July 1981.

3   According to Virginia Baron, 'The Philippine Example', *Fellowship* 53/3 (1987), p. 4, two per cent of the population received fifty-five per cent of the total personal income.

4   My sources for this chapter include the following:
    ● Monina Allaray Mercado (ed.), *An Eyewitness History: People Power, The Philippine Revolution of 1986* (Manila: The James B. Reuter, SJ, Foundation, 1986). Hereafter cited as *People Power*, this magnificent book of eyewitness

104   NON-VIOLENCE, THE INVINCIBLE WEAPON?

accounts and splendid pictures also contains short synopses
of developments and valuable historical notes (pp. 308–314)
on which I have relied for many of the historical details.
- Several articles in the March 1987 issue of *Fellowship* 53/3.
- Peggy Rosenthal, 'Nonviolence in the Philippines: The Pre-
  carious Road', *Commonweal*, 20 June 1986, pp. 364–367.
- Elwood, *Philippine Revolution 1986* (see note 1).
- Bel Magalit, 'The Church and the Barricades', *Transform-
  ation* 3/2 (1986), pp. 1–2.

5 Hildegard Goss-Mayr, 'When Prayer and Revolution Became
   People Power', *Fellowship* 53/3 (1987), p. 9.
6 Quoted in Elwood, *Philippine Revolution, 1986*, p. 19.
7 Mercado, *People Power*, pp. 10, 304.
8 Goss-Mayr, 'When Prayer and Revolution Became . . .', p. 8;
   Rosenthal, 'Nonviolence in the Philippines', p. 366. For earlier
   examples of nonviolence, see Esther Epp-Tiessen, 'Militariz-
   ation and Non-Violence in the Philippines', *The Ploughshares
   Monitor* 7/2 (1986), p. 3 and Richard L. Schwenk, *Onward
   Christians! Protestants in the Philippine Revolution* (Quezon
   City, Philippines: New Day Publishers, 1986), p. 37.
9 Rosenthal, 'Nonviolence in the Philippines', p. 364
10 Quoted *ibid.*, p. 365. See Hildegard Goss-Mayr's account in
   'When Prayer and Revolution Became . . .', p. 9.
11 Quoted in Rosenthal, 'Nonviolence in the Philippines', p. 365.
12 Goss-Mayr, 'When Prayer and Revolution Became . . .', p. 9.
13 *Ibid.*, p. 10.
14 *Ibid.*
15 *Ibid.*
16 See the bishop's official declaration, quoted in Mercado, *People
   Power*, p. 77.
17 *Ibid.*, pp. 43, 67, 68, 71.
18 Quoted *ibid.*, pp. 77–78.
19 Rosenthal, 'Nonviolence in the Philippines', p. 367.
20 Quoted in Elwood, *Philippine Revolution, 1986*, p. 5.
21 Rosenthal, 'Nonviolence in the Philippines', p. 367; Mercado,
   People Power, p. 67.
22 Quoted in Mercado, *People Power*, p. 106.
23 Quoted *ibid.*, p. 105.
24 Quoted *ibid.*
25 Quoted *ibid.*, p. 120.
26 *Ibid.*, pp. 1, 109, 122; and Elwood, *Philippine Revolution, 1986*,
   p. 14.
27 Cited in Mercado, *People Power*, pp. 125–127.
28 Cited *ibid.*, p. 127.
29 Cited *ibid.*, pp. 203–204.

30 Quoted *ibid.*, p. 207.
31 An editorial in the *Philippine Daily Inquirer* 27 February 1986, quoted in Mercado, *People Power*, p. 246.
32 Quoted *ibid.*, p. 254.
33 Vicente T. Paterno, quoted *ibid.*, p. 257.
34 From a statement on Philippine television after the revolution, and shared with me by Melba Maggay, an evangelical Protestant leader deeply involved with the struggle.
35 From his 'Epilogue' in Mercado, *People Power*, p. 306. See Gene Sharp's more cautious but similar comments in 'Philippines Taught Us Lessons of Nonviolence', *Los Angeles Times*, 4 April 1986, Section 2, p. 5. AKKAPKA continues promoting nonviolent social change in the Philippines. See Richard Deats, 'Fragile Democracy in the Philippines', *Fellowship*, Oct.–Nov., 1987, pp. 14–16.

Chapter 4: Multiplying Success

1 Richard B. Deats, 'The Way of Nonviolence', in Thérèse de Coninck (ed.). *Essays on Nonviolence* (Nyack, NY: Fellowship of Reconciliation, n.d.), p. 18.
2 Figures from Walter Wink, *Jesus' Third Way* (Philadelphia: New Society Publishers, 1987), pp. 41–42.
3 *Ibid.*, p. 42.
4 I do serve on WFP's Advisory Board, but I do not mean to suggest that my speech prompted the emergence of WFP later that year.
5 Quoted in de Coninck, *Essays on Nonviolence*, p. 2.
6 Adolfo Perez Esquivel, *Christ in a Poncho: Testimonials of the Nonviolent Struggles of Latin America*, ed. Charles Antoine, trans. Robert R. Barr (Maryknoll, NY: Orbis Books, 1983), p. 32.
7 David A. Hoekema, 'A Practical Christian Pacifism', *The Christian Century*, 22 October 1986, p. 918.
8 I owe this point to Wink, *Jesus' Third Way*, pp. 56–57.
9 Bernard Häring, *The Healing Power of Peace and Nonviolence* (New York: Paulist Press, 1986), pp. 83–84.
10 No. 533 of their declaration, quoted in Esquivel, *Christ in a Poncho*, p. 52.
11 Penny Lernoux, *Cry of the People* (New York: Penguin Books, 1982), p. 447.
12 Quoted in Häring, *Healing Power*, p. 34.
13 Quoted *ibid.*
14 Pastoral Statement of the National Conference of Catholic

Bishops, *The Challenge of Peace: God's Promise and Our Response* (Boston: St Paul Editions, 1983), No. 222, p. 58.

15 *Ibid.*, No. 230, pp. 60–61.

16 The United Methodist Council of Bishops, *In Defense of Creation: The Nuclear Crisis and a Just Peace* (Nashville: Graded Press, 1986), p. 80.

17 National Association of Evangelicals, *Guidelines: Peace, Freedom and Security Studies* (Wheaton, IL: National Association of Evangelicals, 1986), p. 26. See also pp. 3, ii and *passim*.

18 *Ibid.*, p. 28.

19 The concept was first proposed in a speech by Ronald J. Sider at the Mennonite World Conference in Strasbourg, France, in July 1984; the speech was reprinted with the title 'Are We Willing to Die for Peace?' in the *Gospel Herald*, 25 December 1984, pp. 898–901. For the December 1986 gathering, see 'Christian Peacemaker Team Proposal Revised, Approved', *Evangelical Visitor*, February 1987, pp. 14–17. For further information, write to Christian Peacemaker Teams, Peace Section, Mennonite Central Committee, Akron, Pennsylvania 17501.

20 Catholic Bishops, *The Challenge of Peace*, No. 224, p. 58.

21 See further, John Howard Yoder, *When War is Unjust: Being Honest in Just-War Thinking* (Minneapolis: Augsburg, 1984), pp. 76–78.

22 Catholic Bishops, *The Challenge of Peace*, No. 224, p. 59.

23 Gene Sharp, 'The Significance of Domestic Nonviolent Action as a Substitute for International War', in Severyn T. Bruyn and Paula M. Rayman (eds), *Nonviolent Action and Social Change* (New York: Irvington Publishers, 1981), p. 245.

24 For further information, write to The Program on Nonviolent Sanctions, Center for International Affairs, Harvard University, 1737 Cambridge Drive, Cambridge, MA 02138.

25 Both Bernard Häring (*Healing Power*, p. 120) and the US Catholic Bishops (*Challenge of Peace*, No. 228, p. 59) call for new study centres. For a list of current Peace Studies courses in US colleges and universities, see Ronald J. Sider and Richard K. Taylor, *Nuclear Holocaust and Christian Hope* (Downers Grove, IL and Ramsey, NJ: InterVarsity Press/Paulist Press, 1982), pp. 310–311.

26 See Charles C. Walker, *A World Peace Guard* (Hyderabad, India: Academy of Gandhian Studies, 1981), pp. 34, 44, 47–48; Theodore Olson and Lynne Shivers, *Training for Nonviolent Action* (London: Friends Peace Committee, 1970); William Moye, *A Nonviolent Action Manual* (Philadelphia: New Society Press, 1977); Ken Butigan, *et al, Basta! A Pledge of Resistance*

Handbook (San Francisco: Emergency Response Network, undated); Ed Hedemann, ed. *War Resisters League Organizer's Manual* (New York: War Resisters League, 1981); Richard K. and Phyllis B. Taylor and Sojourners, *The Practice of Peace: A Manual and Video for Nonviolent Training* (1987) and available from Sojourners, Box 29272, Washington, D.C. 20017.

27 For a brief discussion of many different non-violent strategies, see Deats, 'The Way of Nonviolence', in de Coninck, *Essays on Nonviolence*, pp. 15–17, and Mubarak E. Awad, 'Nonviolent Resistance: A Strategy for the Occupied Territories', in *Nonviolent Struggle in the Middle East* (Philadelphia: New Society Publishers, n.d.), pp. 28–36. For a much longer, more scholarly analysis, see the superb treatment in Gene Sharp, *The Politics of Nonviolent Action*, 3 vols (Boston: Porter Sargent Publishers, 1973), 2., pp. 117–435.

28 In Wink, *Jesus' Third Way* (see above note 2).

29 See Nat Henthoff, 'Can Israel Create its Own Gandhi, Muste or King?', *Village Voice*, 28 June 1983; the series of articles in the *Jordan Times*, 16–19 November 1986, reporting a conference on non-violence held in Amman; Mubarak E. Awad, 'Nonviolent Resistance: A Strategy for the Occupied Territories' (see note 27); and R. Scott Kennedy, 'The Druze of the Golan: A Case of Nonviolent Resistance', in *Nonviolent Struggle*, pp. 5–21.

30 See Walker, *World Peace Guard*, p. 19.

31 *Ibid.*, p. 25.

32 See the discussion *ibid.*, pp. 13–21.

33 Karl Deutsch, *The Analysis of International Relations* (Englewood Cliffs, NJ: Prentice Hall (1978). See the discussion in the excellent book by Duane K. Friesen, *Christian Peacemaking and International Conflict: A Realist Pacifist Perspective* (Scottdale, PA: Herald Press, 1986), pp. 147–149.

34 Friesen, *ibid.*, p. 148, summarising Gene Sharp.

Chapter 5: The Moral Equivalent of War

1 William James, 'The Moral Equivalent of War', in John K. Roth (ed.), *The Moral Equivalent of War and Other Essays* (New York: Harper & Row, 1971), p. 3. The essay originally appeared in 1910.

2 *Ibid.*, p. 4.

3 Walter Wink, *Jesus' Third Way* (Philadelphia: New Society Publishers, 1987), p. 34.

BIBLIOGRAPHY

Adams, John P. *At the Heart'of the Whirlwind* (New York: Harper & Row, 1976)

Awad, Mubarak E., and R. Scott Kennedy. *Nonviolent Struggle in the Middle East* (Philadelphia: New Society Publishers, 1985)

Bailey, Sydney D. *How Wars End: The United Nations and the Termination of Armed Conflict*, vol. 1 (Oxford: Clarendon Press, 1982)

Bedau, H. A., (ed.). *Civil Disobedience: Theory and Practice* (Nyack, NY: Fellowship of Reconciliation, 1982)

Bondurant, Joan. *Conquest of Violence: The Gandhian Philosophy of Conflict*, revised edition (Berkeley, CA: University of California Press, 1965)

Boserup, Anders, and Andrew Mack. *War Without Weapons: Non-Violence in National Defense* (New York: Schocken Books, 1975)

Bruyn, Severyn T., and Paula M. Rayman, (eds). *Nonviolent Action and Social Change* (New York: Irvington Publishers, 1979)

Camara, Dom Helder. *Revolution Through Peace*, trans. Amparo McLean (New York: Harper & Row, 1971)

de Coninck, Thérése, (ed.). *Essays on Nonviolence* (Nyack, NY: Fellowship of Reconciliation, n.d.)

Conser, Walter H., McCarthy, Ronald M., Toscano David J., and Sharp Gene, (eds). *Resistance, Politics and the American Struggle for Independence, 1765–1775* (Boulder, CO: Lynne Rienner Publishers, 1986)

Desai, Narayan. *Towards Nonviolent Revolution* (India: Sarva Seva Sangh Prakashan, 1972)

Douglass, James W. *The Non-Violent Cross: A Theology of Revolution and Peace* (New York: Macmillan, 1966)

Easwaran, Eknath. *A Man to Match His Mountains: Badshah Khan, Nonviolent Soldier of Islam* (Petaluma, CA: Nilgiri Press, 1984)

Ebert, Theodor. *Soziale Verteidigung* (Waldkirch: Waldkircher Verlagsgesellschaft mbH, 1981)

Elwood, Douglas J. *Philippine Revolution, 1986: Model of Nonviolent Change* (Quezon City, Philippines: New Day Publishers, 1986)

Esquivel, Adolfo Perez. *Christ in a Poncho: Testimonials of the Non-violent Struggles of Latin America*, ed. Charles Antoine, trans. Robert R. Barr (Maryknoll, NY: Orbis Books, 1983)

Friesen, Duane K. *Christian Peacemaking and International Conflict: A Realist Pacifist Perspective* (Scottdale, PA: Herald Press, 1986)

Galtung, Johann. 'Violence, Peace, and Peace Research', *Journal of Peace Research* 3 (1969), pp. 167–191

Gandhi, M. K. *Gandhi: An Autobiography of Mohandas K. Gandhi* (Boston, MA: Beacon Press, 1957)

Haring, Bernard. *The Healing Power of Peace and Nonviolence* (New York: Paulist Press, 1986)

Hope, Marjorie, and Young, James. *The Struggle for Humanity: Agents of Nonviolent Change in a Violent World*. (Maryknoll: Orbis, 1977)

King, Martin Luther. *Stride Toward Freedom* (New York: Harper & Brothers, 1958)

idem. Why We Can't Wait (New York: New American Library, 1963)

Laffin, Arthur J., and Anne Montgomery, (eds). *Swords into Plowshares: Nonviolent Direct Action for Disarmament* (San Francisco: Harper & Row, 1987)

Lakey, George. *Strategy for a Living Revolution* (San Fancisco: W. H. Freeman, 1968)

Lernoux, Penny. *Cry of the People* (New York: Penguin Books, 1982)

Mercado, Monina Allaray, (ed). *An Eyewitness History: People, The Philippine Revolution of 1986* (Manila: the James B. Reuter SJ Foundation, 1986)

Miller, William Robert. *Nonviolence: A Christian Interpretation* (New York: Association Press, 1964)

Millett, Richard. *Guardians of the Dynasty: a History of the US Created Guardia Nacional de Nicaragua and the Somoza Family* (Maryknoll, NY: Orbis Books, 1977)

Oates, Stephen. *Let the Trumpet Sound: The Life of Martin Luther King, JR* (New York: Harper & Row, 1982)

Olson, Theodore, and Shivers, Lynne. *Training for Nonviolent Action* (London: Friends Peace Committee, 1970)

Parkman, Patricia. *Insurrection Without Arms: The General Strike in El Salvador, 1944* (unpublished PhD dissertation, Temple University, 1980)

Pastoral Statement of the National Conference of Catholic Bishops, *The Challenge of Peace: God's Promise and Our Response* (Boston: St Paul Editions, 1983)

Schwenk, Richard L. *Onward Christians! Protestants in the Philippine Revolution* (Quezon City, Philippines: New Day Publishers, 1986)

Sharp, Gene. *Exploring Nonviolent Alternatives* (Boston: Porter Sargent Publishers, 1970)

idem. *Making Europe Unconquerable: The Potential of Civilian-Based Deterrence and Defense* (Cambridge, MA: Ballinger, 1985)

idem. *Making the Abolition of War a Realistic Goal* (New York: Institute for World Order, 1981) (pamphlet)

idem. *The Politics of Nonviolent Action*, 3 vols (Boston: Porter Sargent Publishers, 1973)
Part 1: *Power and Struggle*
Part 2: *The Methods of Nonviolent Action*
Part 3: *The Dynamics of Nonviolent Action*

Sider, Ronald J. *Christ and Violence* (Scottdale, PA: Herald Press, 1979)

Sider, Ronald J., and Taylor, Richard K. *Nuclear Holocaust and Christian Hope* (London: Hodder & Stoughton, 1983)

Snyder, C. Arnold. *The Relevance of Anabaptist Nonviolence for Nicaragua Today* (Akron, PA: Mennonite Central Committee Peace Section, 1984)

Taylor, Richard K. *Blockade: A Guide to Non-Violent Intervention* (Maryknoll, NY: Orbis Books, 1977)

United Methodist Council of Bishops. *In Defense of Creation: The Nuclear Crisis and a Just Peace* (Nashville: Graded Press, 1986)

del Vasto, Lanza. *Warriors of Peace: Writings on the Technique of Nonviolence* (New York: Alfred A. Knopf, 1974)

Walker, Charles C. *Peacekeeping: 1969* (Philadelphia: Friends Peace Committee, 1969)

Walker, Charles C. *A World Peace Guard* (Hyderabad, India: Academy of Gandhian Studies, 1981)

Wallis, Jim, (ed.). *The Rise of Christian Conscience* (New York: Harper & Row, 1987)

Washington, James Melvin (ed). *A Testament of Hope – The Essential Writings of Martin Luther King, JR* (New York: Harper & Row, 1986)

Wehr, Paul. *Conflict Regulation* (Boulder, CO: Westview Press, 1979)

idem. 'Nonviolent Resistance to Nazism: Norway, 1940–45', *Peace and Change: A Journal of Peace Research* 10/3, 4 (1984), pp. 77–95

Windsor, Philip, and Adam Roberts. *Czechoslovakia 1968: Reform, Repression and Resistance* (New York: Columbia University Press, for the Institute of Strategic Studies, London, 1969)

Wink, Walter. *Jesus' Third Way* (Philadelphia: New Society Publishers, 1987)

Witness for Peace Documentation Project. *Kidnapped by the Contras: The Peace Flotilla on the Rio San Juan, Nicaragua, August 1985* (Washington DC: Witness for Peace Documentation Project,

1985) available from Witness for Peace Documentation Project, PO Box 29241, Washington, DC

World Council of Churches. 'Violence, Nonviolence and the Struggle for Social Justice', *The Ecumenical Review* 25/4 (1973)

Yarrow, C. H. Mike. *Quaker Experiences in International Conciliation* (New Haven, CT: Yale University Press, 1978)

INDEX

'people power' 65–71
Petronius (Roman legate) 8–9
Philippines 1, 12, 22, 54–71, 94
Philippines' Catholic bishops'
    pronouncement 63–4
Pinochet (General Augusto
    Pinochet Ugarte) 78
Poland 12, 22, 76
police work 4, 34, 89
Pontius Pilate 7–8
poverty 55–6, 71
power of non-violence 90–2
prayer
    Philippines revolution 61, 65,
        66–7, 68, 70
    in training schemes 85
principles of non-violent
    intervention 87–90
Proano, Leonidas (Bishop) 1
public opinion
    influencing 44–5, 51, 52–3,
        89
    power of 91
Purificacion, Lieutenant
    Colonel 65

Quakers (Society of Friends) 31,
    34, 89
Quainton, Anthony 39
Quisling, Vidkun 20

Ramos, Fidel (General) 64–6,
    69
Reagan, Ronald (President) 35,
    45, 69
Reagan administration 39, 45
religious conflict 4, 16, 28–9,
    88, 89
reporting of atrocities 44–5, 51,
    52–3, 89, 90

revolution
    America 10
    Cuba 76
    India 1
    Nicaragua 38–9, 76
    violent and non-violent 76,
        77–9
Rikhye, Indar Jit 26
Rondon, Candido (Colonel, later
    General) 12
Royden, A. Maude 18–19
Russia 22, 45–6, 78

Salt Campaign 15
Sandinista government 38–40,
    42, 49, 51, 102–3
satyagraha 13, 28, 98
Shanti Sena (Peace Brigade)
    28–9, 30, 32, 88
Sharp, Gene 1–2, 3, 11, 22, 80,
    83
Sheppard, H. R. C. (Canon
    'Dick') 18–19
Sin, Jaime (Cardinal,
    Archbishop of Manila
    64–5, 67, 70
Snyder, Arnold 46–7
Society of Friends (Quakers) 31,
    34, 89
Solidarity 22, 76
Somoza dictatorship 37, 38, 76
South Africa 13, 34, 89
Soviet Union 22, 45–6, 78
Sri Lanka 34, 87
Stalin, Joseph 78
strategies of non-violent
    intervention 87–90
strikes 8, 18, 21–2, 33
study centres 84–5
Syria 26

RONALD J. SIDER

Born in Stevensville, Ontario in 1939, Ron Sider took a degree in history at Yale University, where he also studied for his PhD. A member of the Mennonite Church and a lifelong campaigner for social justice, his spheres of activity have included race relations, voter registration, abortion, third world aid and 'simple living'. He is currently Professor of Theology and Culture at Eastern Baptist Theological Seminary in Philadelphia, Pennsylvania. He is also Executive Director of Evangelicals for Social Action and JustLife, organisations committed to developing and communicating a thoroughly Christ-centred approach to a wide range of social issues.

As an author, Ron Sider has won wide critical acclaim. His first book, *Rich Christians in an Age of Hunger* was described by Michael Green as 'one of the most important books of conscience to be written in recent years.' Of *Nuclear Holocaust and Christian Hope*, which Sider co-authored with Richard Taylor, the late David Watson commented, 'This book contains the most vital challenge facing the Church today. It is one of the most searching and disquieting books I have ever read.'

Ron Sider now lives in Philadelphia with his wife, Arbutus. The couple have two sons and a daughter.